Y0-BYG-883

FORECLOSURES

How to Profitably Invest In Distressed Real Estate

FORECLOSURES

How to Profitably Invest In Distressed Real Estate

by

Andrew James McLean

CONTEMPORARY
BOOKS, INC.
CHICAGO

NOTE: LAWS AND CUSTOMS VARY THROUGHOUT THE COUNTRY

In preparation of this text I have attempted to give good, sound advice in overall strategy and procedure at investing in distressed real estate. By no means am I offering legal advice. While the procedures offered will most likely work in every county of every state, there are some variations in local laws and customs which will require the reader to familiarize himself with.

Due to the huge expanse of our country, complicated further by the fact that half the states use a mortgage as a security instrument, while the other half utilizes a deed of trust, it is impossible in a book of this nature to set down standards of practice for all of them. Although the terms are very similar, and for the most part laws regarding foreclosure and real estate are somewhat uniform nationally, it is sound judgement to consult a trusted real estate attorney or professional in this field to answer specific questions in your area.

For the purpose of clarity, throughout the text I refer essentially to a deed of trust, instead of continually describing both it and a mortgage, when each instrument is mentioned. Although for all practical purposes, both instruments are very similar, the only major difference is their method of enforcement during foreclosure proceedings.

Copyright © 1980 by Delphi Information Sciences Corporation
All rights reserved
Published by Contemporary Books, Inc.
180 North Michigan Avenue, Chicago, Illinois 60601
Manufactured in the United States of America
International Standard Book Number: 0-8092-5695-9

Published simultaneously in Canada by
Beaverbooks, Ltd.
150 Lesmill Road
Don Mills, Ontario M3B 2T5
Canada

This edition published by arrangement
with Delphi Information Sciences Corporation

Contents

CHAPTER I

Introduction

Residential real estate has evolved into the wise investor's tool to overcoming the crippling effects of inflation, and more importantly, a means for the average American to become financially independent, or at best very wealthy. While real estate continues to be a popular investment, there is a certain realm within the category of real estate which has yet to be exploited. It remains almost dormant, awaiting to be pounced upon by the anxious public. It is of course, real estate in foreclosure, or often referred to as distressed property.

Perhaps the mystery that shrouds this specialized field of real estate investment can at best be associated with the Lost Dutchman Mine. The public at large was aware that such a bountiful gold mine existed, either in reality or myth, but nobody seemed to know the exact whereabouts of this hidden cache. Such is the case of real estate in foreclosure, except that the secret to uncovering the gold lining in foreclosure property has been mysteriously kept between a few select investors.

Investment in distressed property has remained a specialized art for a limited few over the years due to a number of reasons. Most evident is the lack of knowledge available to the public on exactly how to get started at investing in foreclosures. Also, the inability of the uninformed public to locate and tap the available supply.

The availability of foreclosure property tends to be somewhat cyclical by nature, varying with conditions of the overal economy. During periods of excessive inflation, similar to those we experienced in the late 1970's and early 80's, associated with excessive

1

appreciation in real estate, the supply of distressed property is reduced from prior periods of recession and reduced appreciation in real estate values. The reason for this is due to two basic factors: high employment and a large amount of equity gained by the homeowner. During these periods of high employment homeowners usually have little difficulty maintaining mortgage payments, whereas during the periods of high unemployment they are faced with reduced income, and thereby have more problems meeting their financial obligations. In addition, during these periods of double-digit inflation, which is usually associated with rapidly increasing real estate values, homeowners gain substantially by the increase in equity in their homes. They can thereby borrow against this equity and defer any short term financial difficulties.

The supply of distressed property will increase dramatically during periods of overall economic instability (recession), which will be associated with a leveling off in real estate values. When this recession begins to erode the economy, recent homeowner's who saved, scrimped, and most likely severely over-extended themselves to acquire their cherished home, will be faced with a difficult financial situation. They anticipated continuing employment and extensive equity growth in their new investment, but during a recession neither of these expectations are very practical. To make ends meet, these recent homeowners must either sell, or allow their homes to be foreclosed upon by lenders.

Prior to the 1973–74 recession, there was inflation, but not the double-digit crippling inflation we face in the 1980's. Also, we are not experiencing an over-supply of housing as we did then. Another major difference is that since that recession, the rate of inflation has been so great that the homeowners of today have a substantial amount of equity in their homes, if they've been fortunate enough to have owned their homes for at least a year or more. This substantial equity position shields the homeowner from the immediate threat of disaster should a change occur in their financial condition. With this equity a homeowner can temporarily borrow against it and avoid an immediate financial calamity.

Then, in a general overview, the supply of foreclosure property will advance when a growth economy subsides into a stage of recession. This occurs when the rate of inflation subsides, the supply of new housing begins to spurt, and due to the lower rate of inflation, homeowner equities also begin to subside.

Investing in foreclosure property requires more research and leg-work than other typical real estate investments. But the extra effort is bountifully rewarded by acquiring property for often much less than its true market value. Thus, as our population continues to expand, and real estate continues to be needed to house those newcomers, the need to restore, rehabilitate, refurbish and relieve the financial burden of those foreclosed upon, will present boundless opportunities for those of you ambitious in distressed property.

ANYONE CAN BUY

No special license is required. You don't have to be a licensed real estate broker or salesman, as long as you're buying for your own purposes. You don't even have to be a citizen of the United States to purchase property in foreclosure. There are no restrictions whatsoever as to who can buy. Information on distressed property is a matter of public record without reserve to anyone.

THE 1980's WILL PRESENT BOUNDLESS OPPORTUNITIES

The last deluge of foreclosure property happened during the 1973–74 recession, as we said earlier, and at that time we also had an over-supply of housing. Such is not the case today. Never before in the United States has such a critical shortage of housing ever occurred.

Skyrocketing interest rates, more and more government regulation, reduced supply of habitable land near major employment centers, and increasing numbers of people requiring adequate housing all help to create the current shortage of housing. In addition, more and more communities are creating legislation to develop rent control programs, which makes matters even worse. The short term effect of rent control appears advantageous, especially for tenants, however the long term result will be disastrous to the future supply of new rentable units. Builders will avoid rent controlled areas like the plague, and erect new housing elsewhere, in areas where such restrictions do not exist. All of these above factors will help add to the value of existing housing during the 1980's market.

Single family homes, by far, will be the most profitable investment during the 1980's. The effects of inflation alone have assured us that single family homes will continue to soar in value. Over the past decade, while the rate of inflation seems almost staggering, the rate of appreciation of single family homes has been one-and-one-half times that rate. In some areas of the country the rate of appreciation has been even greater.

While this rapid increase in the value of single family homes seems never-ending, the magnificent bubble will begin to burst as we head towards an inevitable recession. When it occurs, homeowners who are ill-prepared to endure the hard times will surely lose their cherished homes.

Unfortunate as it may seem, as the recession develops and more and more workers are laid off from the lack of business activity, homeowners will be faced with substantial house payments and other financial obligations. Prior to the impending recession, these homeowners often over-extended themselves and borrowed against the equity in their homes. These loans pledged against their homes were arranged for any number of purposes: perhaps to finance a daughter's higher education, possibly an expensive vacation, a new boat or car, whatever the reason, at the time the logic appeared sound. But now, the homeowner is faced with a reduced earning capacity and something has to go (this is usually the home) into the flow of available foreclosure property.

The majority of homeowners who evolve into the stage of foreclosure will surely lose their property to the lenders, unless by chance they can secure additional funds. Taking into consideration other financial obligations the owner has incurred, along with today's high cost of borrowing (if a lender could be found at all), it is very likely that the distressed homeowner will be unable to avert the eventual foreclosure sale.

Past history has shown that a homeowner who is behind in his house payments, and who in addition owes incidental late charges, will not only end up losing his home, but will lose his good credit rating as well. As unfortunate as it may seem for those who experience this calamity, it is the beginning of almost limitless opportunities for those who are prepared to endeavor at seeking out these distressed properties.

SINGLE FAMILY HOMES . . .
THE BEST PLACE TO BEGIN

A financially rewarding investment career can easily be initiated with a single family home. Neither experience nor huge amounts of capital are required, and nothing else could make an individual feel better about himself than the fact that he owns his own home, or perhaps many properties. Later on, when the investor gains further expertise, he can then begin to invest in additional properties, including multi-unit buildings.

The future appears very bright for those who own single family homes. While demand for them continues to mount, fewer new homes are being built each year. Thus, it can be expected that the rate of appreciation on residential real estate will continue for at least the next twenty years, with the exception of a few minor short-term leveling off periods.

Investing in single family homes is considered to be one of the safest investments available. They can be readily cared for, have the ability to be easily financed compared to other expensive assets, can be insured against all major disasters, and are likely to be sold for a substantial profit.

By far, single family homes are the majority of properties that go through the foreclosure process. Rightly so, there are more single family residences than any other type of real property.

Single family homes are the simplest to purchase. They often can be acquired by assuming the existing financing while securing a grant deed from the owner. You will encounter fewer title and lien complications with this type of property. Additionally, you'll find that acquiring new financing is not as difficult, as you have a wider variety of hospitable lenders, including government backed lenders, as compared to financing larger multi-unit properties.

Besides the ease of acquiring distressed single family homes, they're also easier to rehabilitate, and rent or sell than other types of real property. More families are seeking either to rent or to purchase single family homes than any other form of real estate.

Keep in mind that the availability of real estate in distress tends to be cyclical by nature, increasing in the midst of a recession, and a contraction of the available supply when the overall economy begins to recover. Also, remember that investing in foreclosures is a patient, somewhat analytical endeavor. To be successful it is imperative that you keep abreast of available opportunities, then research and analyze those opportunities to assure you're making a prudent deal. Once you have studied all the material presented in this text, and methodically accomplished all the required analysis and research, you can rest assured that the risk will be absolutely minimized, and that the distressed property you're about to invest in will offer a very rewarding financial opportunity.

REASONS FOR FORECLOSURE

What exactly is "foreclosure"? A definition appropriate for our purposes in this text would be as follows: it is a lawful method of enforcing payment by taking and selling the secured property when the loan is substantially delinquent. Foreclosure is the termination of rights of an owner of real property that is secured by a deed of trust or mortgage, applicable when payment on the debt was not made when it was due.

Why do so many homeowners allow their homes to be foreclosed? Believe it or not, the federal government is inadvertently the culprit at spawning the majority of single family foreclosures. Due to federal home assistance programs, such as VA and FHA, which offer very low or virtually no down payment, a recent homeowner doesn't have much to lose if he cannot meet his mortgage obligation and is foreclosed upon. Under these government programs the buyer merely has to come up with nominal closing costs, and can often move in for less than a $700 investment. All that is required is a fair credit rating and steady employment. (I don't mean to criticize these helpful housing assistance plans. They are definitely a boon to many families who normally could not afford adequate housing. I am merely trying to point out that a lack of adequate homeowner equity often causes the majority of foreclosures.)

In most cases it takes years for this type of buyer to build up equity in his home. If poor financial times come along within two years of the purchase, he feels he hasn't that much to lose since he bought the home with such a small down payment. His attitude might be that he has merely paid rent during that period, or that he has plenty of time to catch up on payments. If the loan is government backed, he can often get away with up to eight or nine months with no loan payments because it will take two to three months just to get a default recorded. During this period he'll receive late notices, payment demands and a variety of collection devices. Only if he totally ignores these will a default be recorded.

By that time the minimum amount of equity acquired in the property will be consumed by the delinquency charges. As time passes the actual foreclosure proceedings are held and he has moved away, leaving the house for that particular government agency to take over. This abandonment, as unappealing as it may be, can be your magnificent gain. We'll discuss later in this text more on how to invest in this type of property.

There are numerous other reasons for foreclosure. Most predominant is when the breadwinner in a household is no longer able to work. The lender will still require regular monthly payments or a notice of default will be recorded.

A divorce in the family will often cause a house to enter the foreclosure process. In this case, the home will be the responsibility of one of the spouses, instead of the responsibility of the two. In which case, the new sole owner might not be accustomed to making the mortgage payments, or in fact he may have difficulty making such payments from his existing income.

A sad event such as a death in the family can cause eventual foreclosure. From all the sadness and remorse, no one may take over the responsibility of making the mortgage payments as a "devil may care attitude" sets over the stricken household.

Income property often faces foreclosure when owners defer maintenance beyond a point of no return. When a property, such as a large apartment building, is not budgeted properly for preventive maintenance, it may physically deteriorate to a point of foreclosure. If a building is not kept up properly, the owner loses income because quality tenants won't continue to stay, therefore he cannot get adequate rent to meet expenses. In order to keep his head above water, he continues making the mortgage payments but does not put any money into keeping up the building. More and more tenants move out. Finally, so many tenants move out and the building deteriorates to the point that the owner cannot continue to make mortgage payments, and foreclosure sale results.

Over-building of new units within a specific area can also cause foreclosure. This can occur when a poorly planned development, like a large housing tract, is being sold off too slowly to meet the cash flow requirements of the developer. The last phase often cannot be completed because of lack of proper financing or, because the developer is having trouble selling the units due to an over-supply in the area by his competitors. The lender will eventually foreclose on the tract, then hire a builder to finish the incompleted homes when the time is appropriate.

The seller of a home who has sold and taken back a second mortgage as partial payment may eventually have to institute a foreclosure proceeding. Should the buyer not make payments on the second mortgage, or on the first, another foreclosure opportunity will present itself to the alert investor.

There are almost an infinite number of reasons for foreclosure, as there are examples. But why do so many homeowners allow their property to be sold out from under them when it can be saved in so many ways? Essentially the reason stems from the distressed homeowner thinking he can save his home at the last moment, and he waits too long to protect his interest. He will continue to ignore the potential trouble until it's too late. While time passes, the delinquency charges continue to add up, the default period elapses, then the foreclosure period begins; and all of a sudden the foreclosure sale results.

These distressed homes can be salvaged by the alert homeowner. Among the many alternatives available, he can outright sell the property, refinance it, take out a new loan, communicate directly with the lender for a postponement, sell other assets, etc. But these procedures take time to act on and unless a timely decision is made by the homeowner, the home will be lost.

CHAPTER 2

The Three Phases of Foreclosure

As an investor of distressed real estate, you will have the choice of investing in any one of three phases which foreclosure property may evolve. The default period is the first phase. The foreclosure proceedings are initiated with a Notice of Default, after which the owner had been sent numerous requests for payments and written threats of eventual foreclosure, should his delinquency condition not be corrected immediately. The Notice of Default is recorded at the request of the lender by the trustee which, in effect, gives notice to the public that the loan is in default. The actual recording of the notice takes place at the County Recorder's Office in the county in which the property is located. It denotes essential data pertaining to the trust deed, the amount in arrears, address of the property, and the date of recording.

In the state of California the trustor (owner) has ninety days from the date of recording the notice of default to reinstate the loan (to make the loan current by paying all payments in arrears, any late charges, or other deficiencies). The law requires the lender to accept the trustor's reinstatement money during this ninety-day period.

If the trustor has not reinstated the loan within the ninety-day reinstatement period, the lender has the right to notify the trustee to publish a Notice of Trustee's Sale on the ninety-first day. This published notice states that the subject property will be sold at public auction to the highest bidder at a given date and place in that county. The actual date of sale will take place at least twenty-one days after the ninety-day reinstatement period.

During this twenty-one day period, referred to as the Publication Period, the lender has the right to refuse reinstatement of the loan and can demand payment in full of the entire unpaid balance of the loan. Often, lenders will allow reinstatement during the Publication Period, depending on past history of the loan, or how the current interest rate compares with the rate attached to the loan in arrears. If the existing rate of interest on the loan is far below that of current market rates, the lender may wish to proceed with the foreclosure sale and re-lend the proceeds out at a higher rate of interest.

It is during the ninety-day default period that the alert investor can enter into negotiations with the troubled owner and acquire the property through various means, which is detailed later in this text.

The second phase is the actual foreclosure sale. It will be a public auction held by the lender, or an agent of the lender, at which the property will be sold to the highest bidder. Proceeds from the sale will be disbursed to all lien holders in order of the priority of their recorded loans. This particular phase of the foreclosure process requires that the successful bidder pay full bid price for the property in cash. This requirement obviously inhibits most novice investors who are usually associated with limited capital to invest.

The third phase in the process of foreclosure proceedings only occurs when the auction is unsuccessful at attaining a buyer at the minimum bid price or higher. The property reverts then to the lender, who is the party that actually begins the bidding with the minimum acceptable bid. If there are no other bidders, the property reverts back to the lender and is placed on his books at a cost of the loan outstanding, including all late fees, trustee fees, and costs associated with the foreclosure sale.

In most cases, a savings and loan or bank is the lender on most real estate transactions, therefore, after an unsuccessful foreclosure sale, they now become owners of the distressed property at a cost of the outstanding loan balance, plus associated charges incurred from the sale. The property is now referred to as Real Estate Owned, or "REO," and is placed on the books at a value of the minimum bid price from the foreclosure sale.

This phase of foreclosure referred to as Real Estate Owned,

wherein a lending institution has taken back a distressed property, offers a variety of opportunity to the wise foreclosure investor. It has been my experience to directly manage over six-million dollars worth of foreclosure property for a major savings and loan in California during the mid 1970's, and for that reason I now offer you some advice from the inside looking out.

REO, as we said, is property that has been foreclosed upon, and which did not sell at public auction. The bank or savings and loan now owns the property. And there is one aspect of REO that makes it a superior investment compared to the other two stages of foreclosure. In the process of acquiring the property, the bank will clear it of all outstanding liens, clear the title, and pay the back taxes, if any. They own it free and clear. If you can acquire REO property, it will be free of problems except deferred maintenance. There are other spectacular advantages to investing in REO property. You can usually purchase REO with a small down payment, and occasionally for virtually no money down. You can finance your purchase at interest rates that are often below market rates, since the lending institution itself is also the seller, and is usually eager to unload the property. It is often possible to defer the first principal and interest payment from one to three months after you acquire title to the property. In addition, it may be possible for you to accomplish some refurbishment while you're in escrow. Finally, the bank will usually handle most of the closing costs (the various costs and fees involved with the act of transferring the property title), since institutional lenders usually have escrow facilities available in-house. Taking these advantages will depend primarily on how good your relation is with the person you're dealing with about REO.

To be successful at investing in REO, it is necessary to find a technique for dealing with the bankers who own it. And this can be difficult because, surprisingly enough, there is a lot of public interest in the purchase of foreclosure property and many potential buyers are constantly inquiring, while the majority are unsuccessful.

Typically, an inquiry from an uninformed member of the public would be in the form of phone calls to various banks, asking if there's foreclosure property available. So many people phone in, the banks now usually give a stock reply: sorry, nothing available.

REO will usually be moved through an established real estate broker, directly to known buyers, or even to personal friends of the banker. Thus, it is your job, if you want to invest in REO, to approach the REO department in person, and to meet its manager. Establishing such a personal relationship at a lending institution is the only viable method of getting into the REO business.

If an REO department is accustomed to handing over their property to a real estate broker, it would then be to your benefit to find out who this broker is and notify him of your interest in REO property.

Besides having the opportunity to manage several millions in foreclosure property for a major savings and loan, one of my most profitable investments was a nineteen-unit apartment building acquired from an REO department. At first glance, it did not appear so desirable. Seven of the nineteen units were vacant, and in dire need of repair. The exterior walls were inscribed with a variety of grafitti, highlighting key members of local neighborhood gangs who nightly would spray-paint their memoirs in various ghastly colors. Due to the numerous vacancies, complicated by the fact that other tenants hadn't paid rent in quite some time, this particular REO department was anxious to sell.

They had earlier foreclosed on this building with an outstanding loan balance of approximately $110,000, which now they agreed would be the selling price. I made a full price offer agreeing to $11,000 down, with the balance financed for thirty years at 8.5% interest. The sellers accepted, contingent upon me buying the property in "as is" condition, where the seller does not warrant anything, and will do no repairs whatsoever. Because I knew that once the property was refurbished, the deadbeats evicted, the vacant units filled with good paying tenants, and it would be worth almost twice what I paid for it, I was anxious to gain control of this potential gold mine.

Opportunities like this are few and far between, although they do exist, they can only be found by the specialist who is continually seeking these hidden opportunities. To site another example, once while I was managing foreclosure property in Southern California, an interesting, timely event occurred. A gentleman walked into my office and inquired if we had any property for sale. Earlier that morning I was informed that we had just taken back, through foreclosure, a dilapidated sixteen-unit building—and what a catastrophe it was. One of the tenants was still on the property and had just called to complain that heavy rains were coming through the ceiling, and that the entire ceiling in her apartment was about to cave in. The timeliness of this event was that the gentleman who appeared in my office inquiring about available property happened to be a roofing contractor.

I told him of the available sixteen-unit building, which was presently being inundated by a major storm. He said he'd drive out and take a look at it, and see what he could do.

Later that day he returned and stated that a three-inch wide by fifteen-foot long gap existed in the roof, and water was gushing into the building. He had laid a polyethelene cover over the gap, then masked it down, which would temporarily keep the water out.

Since the building would obviously require much repair, and we would prefer not owning it, I offered it to him for what my company had in it, an outstanding loan balance of $72,000. He accepted, and both parties were very well satisfied with the transaction. My company sold a real loser, and by doing so was able to avoid sinking new money into a dilapidated building. On the other hand, the investor can make something of the property with some investment and elbow grease. Besides, the savings and loan I worked for was not in the business of investing in real estate. Their primary function is to take in deposits, then re-lend those deposits to borrowers at a profit.

The point I'm trying to bring across is that profitable opportunities do not simply grow on trees waiting to be picked like a ripe plum. You have to make a concentrated effort to locate, then develop those opportunities. Otherwise, those who are making the effort will buy those profitable opportunities right out from under your nose, while you're waiting around watching the plum grow.

PROCEDURES FOR ACQUIRING PROPERTIES

We have already discussed the opportunities available during the three phases of foreclosure. In the first phase, the Default Period, you'll have the opportunity to work with distressed owners prior to the actual foreclosure sale in an attempt to acquire the property. If by chance you are fortunate enough to be endowed with a surplus of cash, then you'll have available resources to purchase foreclosures during the second phase, at the actual foreclosure sale. Or, perhaps you like the idea of working with institutional lenders and prefer investing in distressed property during its third phase, when it becomes Real Estate Owned of the lender who foreclosed.

Before really digging in and discussing the details of available approaches you may wish to take, it is essential to your success that the terminology used in this specialized field of foreclosure be clarified, and that you follow these overall steps to acquiring properties.

1. LEARN THE TERMINOLOGY. It is important for you to become knowledgeable with the procedures and terminology involved with the process of foreclosure so that you can portray yourself as a knowledgeable person to the owners of the property you will be dealing with. This, in turn, will make it easier for you to function efficiently and effectively at acquiring worthwhile investments.

2. ACQUAINT YOURSELF WITH SOURCES OF DISTRESSED PROPERTY. Essentially, you have four available sources in which to tap for property in distress: Real Estate Owned, which is foreclosure property taken back by an institutional lender; legal newspapers and fee subscription services, which publish defaults and foreclosure sale notices, and the County Recorder's Office which records notices relevant to our subject.

3. DECIDE ON A SPECIFIC TERRITORY TO OPERATE IN. It is next to impossible to become an expert on real estate in distress when the area of concentration is too large. Therefore, it is better to concentrate your efforts in a specific small area where you can learn property values, keep tabs on events which may affect values, and acquaint yourself with people who can be helpful in that area.

4. PREPARE A LIST OF POTENTIAL INVESTMENTS. Now that you're acquainted with your territory and have tapped various sources of distressed property, you can begin to narrow down, through the process of elimination, those properties which show a good profit potential.

5. PREPARE AN INVESTMENT ANALYSIS. Once you have narrowed down a number of properties which should be given further consideration, a careful analysis is made to determine what kind of offer you will make to the prospect.

6. MEET AND NEGOTIATE WITH THE OWNER. Here a mood of mutual assistance will be portrayed by the specialist investor. Procedures will be fully explained to the distressed owner. You will stress the fact that only the specialist investor can truly remedy the distressed owner's precarious situation.

7. ESTIMATING THE COSTS. Now that all the relevant facts about the property have been revealed by the troubled owner, you can estimate all the costs involved and prepare for the next step.

8. CLOSING THE DEAL. During this phase you will be acquainted with the various forms necessary to close the deal and how to complete them inexpensively.

9. WHAT TO DO ONCE YOU OWN THE PROPERTY. Now, in the final phase, you will have the opportunity to do any one of three things with your newly acquired investment: sell at a profit, then reinvest the profits, or refinance it to buy additional property, or trade your property for one of higher value.

LEARN THE TERMINOLOGY

What is foreclosure? By definition it is the procedure where property pledged for security for a debt is sold to pay the debt in the event of default in payment and terms. The process varies from state to state, but essentially the procedure is usually similar throughout the country. The major difference in procedures is between states who use a mortgage as security on real property, and those who use a deed of trust.

Mortgages and Deeds of Trust

Mortgages and deeds of trust are written instruments which create liens against real property. Should the borrower default on the loan (fail to make payments when due), mortgages and trust deeds will allow the lender to sell the property in order to satisfy the loan obligation.

The two parties involved in a mortgage are referred to as the *Mortgagor,* who is the property owner or borrower, and the *Mortgagee,* or lender. There are two parts to a mortgage: the *Mortgage Note,* which is evidence of the debt, and the *Mortgage Contract,* which is security for the debt. The Note promises to repay the loan, while the Contract promises to convey title of the property to the Mortgagee in case of default.

Should the Mortgagor fail to make payments, the property can then be sold through foreclosure in a court action. In order to do so the Mortgagee must first obtain from the court a foreclosure judgement, which orders the sheriff to sell the property to the highest bidder (over and above what is due the lender). The property is then put up for public auction. Should a successful bid be made, the bidder receives from the sheriff a document known as the *Certificate of Sale.* The bidder must then hold the certificate for one year before he will be issued the deed to the property. If, within that year, the Mortgagor pays the bidder sufficient monies (bid price plus interest), the Mortgagor then retains ownership of the property and the foreclosure sale is nullified. The period during which a Mortgagor is entitled to redeem his property is referred to as the *Mortgagor's Equity of Redemption.*

Trust Deeds are similar to mortgages except that: a) an additional third party is involved, and b) the foreclosure period is much shorter.

With a trust deed, the property owner or borrower is called the *Trustor,* and the lender is the *Beneficiary.* The intermediate party, whose job it is to hold title to the property for the security of the lender, is called the *Trustee.*

Should the Trustor default on his loan obligation, the subject property will be sold by the Trustee at public auction through a "power of sale" clause contained in all trust deeds, without court procedure.

Foreclosure is initiated by a *Notice of Default,* which is recorded by the Trustee, with a copy sent to the Trustor. After three months, a Notice of Sale is posted on the property, and an advertisement for sale is carried in local newspapers once a week for three weeks. If during this period the Trustor fails to pay the

Beneficiary sufficient funds to halt the foreclosure (overdue loan payments, plus interest, penalties and fees), the sale will then be conducted by the Trustee. Proceeds from foreclosure are disbursed to the Beneficiary, then to any other lien holders.

Throughout America, approximately half the states still use the traditional mortgage as security for real estate loans, while a few states use both the mortgage and a deed of trust as a security instrument. Although lenders prefer the deed of trust overall, due to the fact that a foreclosure can be effected in one-third the time of a traditional mortgage, and without court action.

Again, I would like to state that throughout this text I refer only to deeds of trust. The reason for doing so is to simplify the text so it isn't necessary to discuss both instruments in each chapter and subchapter. Both the deed of trust and mortgage serve the same purpose, the only major difference is the method of enforcement in the case of default.

The following are additional terms you should be familiar with.

Assignment of Deed of Trust
A written financial document which transfers rights of the Beneficiary of a Deed of Trust to another party.

Substitution of Trustee
A written document, often located on the back of a deed of trust, which transfers trusteeship. Transfer or substitution of trustees are made for reasons of convenience, more personal service, etc. Legally, the Beneficiary can also be the Trustee. His purpose in doing so might be to gain control of a trustee sale.

Notice of Action (Lis Pendens)
A legal notice that a lawsuit is pending on the subject property. It gives notice that anyone acquiring an interest in the subject property after the date of notice may be bound by the outcome of the pending litigation.

Obviously, you should be very careful with such a notice attached to a property you're interested in. Unlike most other liens and attachments, a foreclosure sale usually does not wipe out this pending litigation.

Rescission

The act of nullifying the foreclosure process. It places the property back to its previous condition, before the default was recorded. Recordation of a rescission removes the default from the title records.

Power of Sale

The power of sale clause is written into all deeds of trust, giving the trustee the right to advertise and sell the secured property at public auction if the trustor defaults on the loan. This power of sale clause enables the trustee to sell the property without court order. When the sale is completed at the public auction, the trustee will convey title to the purchaser, use the funds from the proceeds to satisfy the beneficiary, then return surplus monies, if any, to the trustor. Once all this is accomplished, the trustor is entirely divested of his property without any right of redemption.

ACQUAINT YOURSELF WITH THE SOURCES

Sources of information regarding real estate in foreclosure are available through a variety of outlets. Services that provide such information vary throughout the country due to each state's legal requirements. Some states require the Notice of Default to be publicized in a legal newspaper. Many legal newspapers publish notices of default simply as a community service.

In addition to legal newspapers, some companies make available public record services on a fee subscription basis. Both legal newspapers and fee subscription services attain their information directly from the County Recorder's office. Their published information is rearranged into a more easily read form. The cost of this convenient service is substantially higher than that of legal newspapers, or the free information available from the public records or the County Recorder.

Of course, you could get information on recorded defaults directly from the County Recorder. This data is recorded daily and available for public use.

Once the default on a deed of trust has been recorded and the 90-day redemption period has elapsed, the Trustee is legally required to publish the Notice of Trustee Sale. This legal notice *cannot* be found at the County Recorder's office because the trustee is only required to publish, not record this notice. You can attain this information from subscription services, legal newspapers, and often in local newspapers which are authorized to publish these legal notices. Further legalities require the Trustee to post the Notice of Trustee Sale on one or more public buildings within the same county and on the subject property itself. Thus, you'll often notice these postings on bulletin boards in your county court house.

Keep in mind that these services which publish notices of default are not liable for the accuracy of the information they publish. It is not uncommon to find incorrect addresses or other data published by such services. The only data that can be deemed reliable are the actual recordings found in the County Recorder's office.

The majority of this vital information about the default could be attained by ordering preliminary title reports from a title company. Needless to say, it is quite expensive. In order for you to become a professional specialist in the field of distressed property, you should examine the records available at no expense at the County Recorder's office. By doing so you can gain the experience necessary to be an expert in this field.

It should further be noted that these published services do not state whether the instrument in default is a first, second, or third deed of trust. To correctly determine which of the liens is in default, you'll have to make a personal visit to the County Recorder's office and look it up yourself.

Occasionally, these legal notices of default omit the exact street address of the subject property. If this is the case, you can get the correct address by consulting the map books available while you're at the County Recorder's office. This can be attained by matching the given legal description with those in the available map books.

Once you attain needed information about a distressed property and you decide to pay a visit to the property, you'll note an interesting phenomena. Property in foreclosure, ninety-nine times out of a hundred, always has the same appearance. You can spot the neglected property a mile away. It's the only house on the block with a dried out, unmowed lawn with debris scattered about. You may notice a broken window or two, possibly a roof in need of repair, and it may require some paint. These "tattered ladies" stand out in the neighborhood like a pair of polka dot tennis shoes worn with a tuxedo.

There was a time when the Trustee would offer necessary information about the default to the public as a professional courtesy. This service, unfortunately is not given so freely any more, due to the increasing popularity among speculators in this interesting field. Today, besides holding a public auction on the subject property, the trustee is not obligated to provide information, except for date, time, and location of the sale. (See sample of a published notice of default on the next page.)

DECIDING ON A SPECIFIC
TERRITORY IN WHICH TO OPERATE

For the purpose of efficiency, it is important that you restrict your operations to a specific area within your city. The area you select could appropriately be in the neighborhood where the investor is a resident. The major reason for working within a certain designated area is to develop both contacts in that area, and to get to know property values so that you can quickly ascertain market value in order to expedite an efficient sale. The area you select should have the potential of growth which will eventually lead to an increase in property values.

Once the territory has been selected, you can begin accumulating data relevant to events occurring in the area. You can procure a large map of the area and then note sales prices of homes, where schools are located, and specific streets where resales offer higher dollars per square foot of house. Additionally you can note areas that show signs of reduced value, possibly due to crime or poor land planning, or traffic jams in the area.

When you become a specialist in this territory, you don't have to confine your activities to single family residences. Get to know values of income property, raw acreage and industrial projects.

Limit your territory to an area not to exceed 2,000 homes. A large map of the area can be attained from the County Assessor or

PUBLISHED NOTICE OF DEFAULT

NOTICE OF DEFAULT AND ELECTION TO
SELL UNDER A DEED OF TRUST

Loan No. MI-XXXXXXXXX

Foreclosure No. S-XXXXXX

Original 'Notice of Default' recorded 7-9-78,
File No. 78-46 XXXXX, in Office of Recorder
of Los Angeles County, California.

NOTICE IS HEREBY GIVEN:

That XXXXXXXXFEDERAL SAVINGS AND
LOAN ASSOCIATION , a corporation, is Trustee
under a Deed of Trust executed by XXXXXXXX
and dated January 3, 1975, and recorded January
I4,1975, page no. 472, Document No. XXXXXX
Book XXXXXX, of Official Records in the Office of the Recorder of the County of Los Angeles,
State of California, and given to secure payment
of a promissory note for $10,670.20, dated January
3,1975, payable with interest thereon and therein
provided, in favor of XXXXXXX FEDERAL
SAVINGS AND LOAN ASSOCIATION, a
corporation.

That a breach of the obligations for which said
Deed of Trust was given as security has occurred
in that the following payments due upon said note
were not paid when due, and still remain due,
owing, and unpaid:

The monthly installment of principal
due March 1, 1978, and subsequent
installments thereafter, thereby decl-
aring the entire principal balance of
$8,974.66 due and payable, and late
charges as set forth in said Deed of
Trust, and together with any and all
sums advanced by the Beneficiary
under the terms and provisions of
said Deed of Trust, and delinquent
taxes, assessments, and insurance premiums, if any.

That by reason thereof, the undersigned,
present beneficiary under said Deed of Trust, has
executed and delivered to said Trustee a written
declaration of default and demand for sale, and
has surrendered to said Trustee said Deed of
Trust and all documents evidencing obligations
secured thereby, and has declared and does
declare all sums secured thereby immediately
due and payable, and has elected and does hereby
elect to cause the property described in said
Deed of Trust to be sold to satisfy the obligations secured thereby.

NOTICE

You may have the right to cure the default
described herein and reinstate the mortgage or
deed of trust. Section 2924c of the Civil Code
permits certain defaults to be cured upon the
payment of the amounts required by that section without requiring payment of that portion
of principal and interest which would not be due
had no default occurred. Where reinstatement is
possible, if the default is not cured within three
months following the recording of this notice,
the right of reinstatement will terminate and the
property may be sold.

To determine if reinstatement is possible and
the amount, if any, necessary to cure the default,
contact the beneficiary or mortgagee or the successors in interest, whose name and address as of
the date of this notice is: XXXXXXXFederal
Savings and Loan Association of Los Angeles
(Mailing Address: XXXXXXXXXXXXXXXXX
XXXXXXXX

Dated   March 21,1978

Lot 7, Block 13, Tract XXXXX, as per map
recorded in Book XXXX, Pages XXX through
76, except the Northerly 35 feet thereof,
County of Los Angeles, State of California.
XXXXXXXFEDERAL SAVINGS AND LOAN
ASSOCIATION OF XXXXXXXXXXXXXXX

By XXXXXXXXXX

Assistant Secretary

the County Clerk's office. Make notations on your map in pencil denoting trends and events as they occur, either positively or negatively, that may have an economic impact on your designated territory.

PREPARE A LIST OF POTENTIAL INVESTMENTS

This procedure begins with narrowing down the total supply of distressed property available which you have compiled from various sources. Start with all Real Estate Owned available which you have attained after meeting with REO managers. Then compile available property through the sources spoke of earlier: that of legal publications, subscription services, and the county recorder's office.

Compile all pertinent data on each property on the Property Information sheet. (See sample copy on next page.) This form lists all the vital information which you will need to make a financial analysis and close the deal effectively.

Additional potential investments can be developed while the foreclosure investor is becoming acquainted with his specific territory. Quite often, signs of property that will eventually be in a distressed condition can be spotted by one with an alert eye. Rundown homes which have debris scattered about are usually rented out by absentee landlords. Due to varying circumstances, they are often abandoned by the tenants, and the absentee landlord should be contacted immediately to procure a sale. Absentee landlords who own vacated property often board up the windows and doors to protect their property from vandals. If you spot a boarded home which is not already on your list, find out who the owner is and try and make a deal.

PREPARE AN INVESTMENT ANALYSIS

Now that a list of potential investments has been made, it is time to prepare a financial analysis of those that deserve further consideration. From the Property Information Sheet, more detailed information can be gathered and noted on this form.

PROPERTY INFORMATION SHEET

Lot No. _____ Block No._____

Map page No. _____

Owner's Name: _____

Property address: _____

Phone: [Home] _____ [Work] _____

Date default action taken: _____ Final date to correct _____

First loan
Lender's name: _____ Loan No: _____
Type: _____ Is it assumable? _____ Rate of interest: _____
Original principal owing: _____ Balance as of: _____
Is _____ Monthly payments _____ Annual taxes _____

Second loan
Lender's name: _____ Loan No.: _____
Type: _____ Is it assumable? _____ Rate of interest: _____
Original principal owing: _____ Balance as of: _____
Is _____ Monthly payments _____

Payments in arrears
First loan _____ No. of months at _____ = _____
Second loan _____ No. of months at _____ = _____
Third loan _____ No. of months at _____ = _____
Total late charges = _____
Total default and foreclosure fees = _____
Total amount in arrears as of _____
Description of other liens
1. _____ as of _____ total owing incl. penalties _____
2. _____ as of _____ total owing incl. penalties _____

Sq. Footage of liveable area _____ Lot size _____
No. of bedrooms _____ No. of baths _____ Dining _____ Garage _____
Estimated cost to repair interior (describe rooms & work required) _____
_____

Total estimated cost of interior and exterior: _____
Property location factors (Good, average, below average): _____
Lot: _____ Shopping _____ Public transportation _____
Schools _____ Parks & other _____ Freeways _____

Preliminary cost estimates
Total cost of all delinquencies = _____
Title & escrow expenses = _____
Loan transfer or origination fee = _____
1 month's P&I and taxes & insurance = _____
Cash required for additional liens = _____
Total cash required to make current = _____
Total interior & exterior repair costs = _____

Reason for the default, date of the default notice, final date to correct the default, and all necessary financial data, plus a range of value of what the property would be worth in good condition should be noted at this time. This will take us to the next step which is to contact the owner.

MEET AND NEGOTIATE WITH THE OWNER

It should be kept in mind at all times that the purpose of your visit to the property is not only to aid the troubled owner in his distressed situation, but also to make a good deal for yourself. If everything goes according to the plan, the troubled owner will receive cash for his equity and his credit will be salvaged, while you acquire title to the property.

You should refrain from using the phone until an actual meeting with the owner has been accomplished. This will avoid the potential of the troubled owner brushing you off easily over the phone. A personal visit not only is more business like, but it will also offer you the opportunity of looking over the home.

Begin your approach with a simple introduction of who you are and why you're there, suggesting a mood of mutual assistance. Mention that you have discovered through your sources that his property might be for sale. If, in fact the property is for sale, you can immediately get into the details of the transaction. However, should the troubled owner not currently have the property up for sale, a different approach has to be used.

Time is definitely of the essence in dealing with distressed property which is in the foreclosure process.

The Time Element in Distressed Property

It is important for you to understand that investment in foreclosure property is a patient business. There is much effort, analysis of pertinent data, and continuing effort in order to keep abreast of available opportunities.

Remember, that time is on the side of you, the investor. The pressure is on the distressed owner for him to remedy his situation, or else he will lose the property and his good credit rating. It is to your advantage to remind the distressed homeowner that you're interested in making a good deal for yourself, while at the same time helping the owner in realizing some cash and salvage his credit rating.

During the periods of stress which these distressed homeowners face during foreclosure proceedings, it is important for you to remember that they often disguise the truth about certain matters. Understandably so, the loss of home and property is obviously a stressing condition to be faced with. Therefore, it is imperative that all details of what the distressed homeowner says be verified. While you're in the presence of the homeowner it is essential for you to keep the dialogue going to find out as much as possible about his financial condition, and the house.

Should the distressed owner miraculously remedy his financial condition and bring his delinquent payments up to date, be happy for him. But at the same time continue to keep him in touch, because now the homeowner is faced with an additional problem; How to keep up with the existing house payments plus paying back the additional funds he borrowed to remedy his initial crisis. Chances are, that by continuing to keep in touch with him, the opportunity to make a deal on the property will arise once again.

The following are suggested opening conversational bits which you can use to stimulate negotiations with the distressed owner.

"If you'll allow me to make a complete financial analysis of the property, I can be back within 24 hours with a firm offer which will solve your current dilemma."

"By assisting you during these troubled times, I can help myself at the same time."

"I can operate much faster than a real estate agent, plus save you a costly sales commission."

"I completely understand how you feel. By allowing me to acquire your property you can be assured that the lender, or anyone else, cannot profit from your hard luck."

"My purpose in being here is to offer you cash for your equity which you would lose in a foreclosure sale. Therefore, by dealing with me you can salvage your good credit and drive away much better off and start all over again."

"Please allow me to see the documents on your home. Do you have the deed, the title policy and the payment records?"

"Be careful you do not let other people know that we are speaking about a deal. If brokers and lenders get involved it could make our deal very messy."

It is important at the onset of negotiations that the owner is made aware that time is of the essence. Since he is in the midst of a foreclosure proceeding, care should be taken that the deal is completed before it is too late.

Often, during initial stages of negotiating with the troubled owner, he might mention that he's arranging new financing on his distressed property. He somehow believes that the current situation can be alleviated by acquiring additional funds. The important point for you to remember is that when a house is in foreclosure, most likely the owner will be unable to acquire additional financing. It is unlikely lenders would underwrite an additional loan with the current loan(s) in default. Since the owner cannot make payments on the first loan, he probably won't be able to make payments on another loan, either.

If by chance he is able to get a loan from someone, he's probably only postponing the inevitable foreclosure, because he now has to maintain additional loan payments on top of the loan he is already in default on.

Then, should the distressed owner state that he is arranging another loan, advise him like this: "Okay, if you feel supplemental funds will ease your distressed situation, then by all means do it. But if you cannot arrange the loan, or if you have problems later, please call me so that I may present an offer for your house and assist in rectifying your credit."

The important point at this time is to leave the owner with a positive view of you, as an investor who wants to help, so that if he gets into a distressed situation, he knows who to call.

As a professional investor you can act faster and offer more results to a distressed owner than anyone else. The real estate agent who gets involved in the transaction requires the expense of a sizable commission, which is a needless expense when you, the private investor, purchase the property. Should government agencies get involved, they'll require expensive repairs and timely applications to be filled out before money will be funded.

The Best Prospect in Town

A run-down shabby house will always be the best deal in town. In fact, the more run-down the better. Each and every defect in the condition of a home offers opportunity to the wise distressed property investor. Every problem can be turned into more profit for the investor. Each defect with the house must be noted, then a minimum and maximum price must be estimated to correct each defect. Then the deal with the distressed owner is made on the basis of the maximum repair cost estimate plus a good profit for the investor. Once the property is acquired, maximum effort must be made to refurbish the property at a price as close to the minimum cost estimate as possible.

It is not of major importance for the investor to be a jack-of-all-trades and to fix everything himself, but it is essential that the investor be accurate at discovering problems and know how much it will cost to repair each problem. Then, it will be necessary for the investor to know what the reconditioned home will sell for in that particular neighborhood. It is obviously foolish to invest in a property if the total cost of refurbishment is greater than its market value.

It would be a good practice to know a contractor who can walk through a home with you and determine the soundness of such items as the roof, overall plumbing, and the foundation. Be thorough in your initial examinations. After a time and a few walk-throughs with someone you've hired to inspect, you will gain enough experience that you can make the same analysis yourself.

By thoroughly checking out the entire property, making a careful analysis, then honestly evaluating the sales price of the property once work is completed, you can rest assured that the risk has been minimized and a profit will be realized. If by chance after a careful analysis was made and the numbers simply did not work out, and the total costs of refurbishment are more than the resale value, don't entirely maroon the project. Go back to the troubled owner and open negotiations for a new deal. Point out that it is necessary for you to make a reasonable profit. If you're still unable to make a good deal for youself, then it's time to pack your bags. Chances are, that if you keep in touch every three months or so, the same owner will be faced with financial difficulty once again. Keep the information you've compiled filed away because the information you just attained may be useful someday in the future.

ESTIMATING THE COSTS

About the easiest way to acquire a property in foreclosure is to assume the existing loan while making up all loan payments in arrears, then purchasing the deed from the owner, and finally takeing possession. Very neat and clean. But more often than not, it will be necessary to involve yourself with details that tend to complicate matters involving distressed property.

In order to simplify matters, a cost estimate sheet follows which takes into consideration all items involved when investing in foreclosed property. It is imperative that you write down all costs to eliminate potential errors.

PURCHASING THE DEED

Make certain that the owner (grantor) has the property vested in his name. To verify these, check the grant deed or the title insurance policy. If none of these are available, check the escrow documents when the owner purchased the property. If none of the above three are available for verification, check the official records at the County Recorder's office.

You must know the difference between a Grant Deed and a Quitclaim Deed. When an owner of real property issues a Grant

COST ESTIMATE SHEET

Address _____

Cost of Acquiring Property:
    Purchasing the Deed $_____
    Delinquent Taxes   _____
    Bonds & Assessments   _____
    Delinquencies on 1st Loan:
      _____ months @ $_____   _____
    Total Late Charges & Fees   _____
    Advances   _____
    Pay off Second Loan (include
      all delinquencies, advances
      and fees).   _____
Preliminary Cost Estimates:
    Title & Escrow expenses   _____
    Loan Transfer or Origination Fee   _____
    1 month P&I and Taxes & Ins.   _____

Total Cash to Purchase   ==========
    Balance of all loans after purchase   _____
    Other Encumbrances   _____

Total Property Cost (before repairs)   ==========
Cost of Repairs Needed:

Paint _____	Plumbing _____	Roof _____
Electrical _____	Termite _____	Fencing _____
Landscape _____	Floors _____	Carpeting _____
Wallpaper _____	Fixtures _____	Hardware _____

    Total Cost of Repairs   ==========

    Total Property Cost   ==========
      (after repairs)

Deed, he is warranting that he has marketable title to the property. A Quitclaim Deed simply releases any interest the grantor may have in the property. If the grantor has no interest in the property, he is not releasing anything. For example, assume you give me a Quitclaim Deed on the Brooklyn Bridge. Although you may not have any interest in the Brooklyn Bridge whatsoever, you are simply executing a statement to that fact saying "I have no interest whatsoever in the Brooklyn Bridge." Obviously you have no interest in it, therefore, you are releasing nothing. When you receive a Quitclaim Deed it is imperative that the grantor has an interest that is conveyed to you.

Real Estate Taxes

It is not uncommon for a property to have delinquent property taxes assessed against it, and occasionally up to three years worth could have accumulated. This is often the case when the lender does not make provisions for an impound account for hazard insurance and property taxes. The purpose of the impound account is to allow the borrower to pay a prorated share of these expenses monthly into a trust out of which the lender pays these liabilities. In the event you are dealing with properties that have VA or FHA loans on them, you can be assured that the taxes are fairly up to date because these government backed loans provide for an impound account.

The best method of making sure the property taxes have been paid is to get the information directly from your County Tax Collector. All that is required is a simple phone call if you can supply the Tax Collector with the complete legal description of the subject property. If that is not available, a personal visit to the County Tax Collector will be required.

Bonds and Assessments

Most frequently, these items show up in less than fully developed areas where sewers and sidewalks have not been completed.

Be very careful of these liens against real property because they do not always appear on the title report. These liens are recorded against real property and are written in a way to allow the home-owner to pay them off monthly over a period of years. However, in some cases, these bonds and assessments have to be fully paid off when the property is sold.

To verify if any of these forms of liens are outstanding, or any other details about them, a phone call to the Tax Department or the County Treasurer will resolve these matters.

WHAT ABOUT THE EXISTING LOANS?

Probably the most important consideration in purchasing a property in foreclosure is the existing loan, or secondary loans, if any. Due to the fact that there are a variety of methods in which the property could have been financed, we must first discuss these various methods which you will encounter.

Conventional financing refers to a method of lending on real estate when VA and FHA government backed loans are *not* involved. Here an institutional lender, such as a bank or savings and loan, would typically lend 75 to 80% of the appraised value of the home being purchased. These conventional loans are made on more of a conservative basis than VA and FHA loans, they involve higher interest rates, prepayment penalties, and most have "due-on-sale clauses."

Conventional loans usually have a provision for a prepayment penalty. This refers to a situation where the lender has the right to charge a penalty if the loan is paid off before maturity. This penalty can vary depending on the lender, but is usually six to nine months interest on the unpaid principal balance.

In addition, most conventional loans have "due-on-sale" clauses or an "acceleration clause" written into the loan agreement. This is a provision giving the lender the right to call all monies owed him to be immediately due and payable upon the happening of a certain stated event. The certain stated event usually refers to transfer of ownership without the lender's approval.

The Wellencamp Case in California

In the state of California, prior to August 25, 1978, it was next to impossible for a new buyer to assume the existing first trust deed of another borrower when a conventional loan was involved. In a direct purchase when the new buyer wished to take over the existing loan, most lenders would insist on writing a new loan at a much higher interest rate and monthly payment. But in August of 1978 the State Supreme Court ruled that lenders can no longer increase interest rates on existing real property loans unless the lender has been penalized.

Now, with the advent of the Wellencamp decision, the public is becoming aware that investors can purchase a property subject to its first deed of trust. Then, an investor can prevent the bank from acquiring the property through foreclosure by making the loan current and taking title to the distressed property, while at the same time salvaging the owner's credit rating and a portion of his equity.

Nonconventional Loans

Nonconventional loans are in the form of VA and FHA government backed loans. The VA loan is extended to qualified veterans, entitling them to borrow money for homes, mobile homes and farms, with 100% financing at lower than market interest rates. VA loans are underwritten and processed by conventional lenders, but a portion of the loan is guaranteed by the Veteran's Administration against default.

FHA loans are also government backed loans, under the supervision of the Federal Housing Administration. They are not restricted to veterans but are also available to other individuals who meet the requirements of the FHA. An FHA loan is underwritten and processed by conventional lending institutions, as with the VA loan, and the lender is similarly insured against default by the buyer. Thus, the lender is able to grant more lenient terms, so that FHA loans offer a lower interest rate and smaller down payment than conventional financing.

Both VA and FHA loans offer the foreclosure investor much

more latitude than that of conventional loans. This is due mainly to the fact that these loans can easily be assumed by the new buyer without any qualification whatsoever; as opposed to some conventional loans, the existing interest rate is maintained, rather than adjusted upwards to reflect the current market rate of interest. Furthermore, these government backed loans usually do not have a provision for a prepayment penalty if the loan is at least two years old.

Obviously, from what we have covered so far, you can see that when you deal with property that has either a VA or FHA loan attached, it will be much easier for you to take over the existing financing. In the event the property you are interested in has a conventional loan on it, you will be faced with negotiating directly with the lender. Often, conventional lenders will charge a 1 to 2% assumption fee on the unpaid balance. Plus, they will probably adjust the interest rate upwards to equal the current market rate of interest.

Conventional lenders vary substantially in their methods of handling delinquencies. Normally, conventional lenders are much more strict about allowing a borrower to fall in arrears on his payments. They will usually record a notice of default if the borrower falls 60 to 90 days in arrears on his payments. VA and FHA lenders usually are more patient with the borrower and often wait up to six months before recording a notice of default.

Additionally, conventional lenders normally charge higher late charges on a delinquent loan than does the VA or FHA. These late charges can run as high as 1/10 of 1% on the unpaid balance per month.

The law provides the borrower a period of reinstatement of the loan, which means within a certain period the loan can be reinstated (brought up to date), when all monies in arrears are paid in full, plus all penalties. This period of reinstatement varies from state to state.

When a homeowner allows his home-loan to go into arrears to the extent that the lender records a notice of default and foreclosure proceedings begin, he is usually required to pay a sizeable sum to make the loan current. And, due to the substantial amount required to make the loan current, it is very probable that the homeowner will have to either sell, or allow the lender to foreclose on his home.

In conclusion of this chapter, if you invest in a property which has a VA or FHA loan attached, you'll benefit from the following: a) You can assume the existing loan without credit qualification. b) You can assume the existing loan for a small incidental fee. c) You won't be charged a prepayment penalty when you sell. d) The interest rate will remain the same throughout the term of the loan. e) You can allow the next buyer to assume all the same benefits.

If you invest in a property which has a conventional loan and a due-on-sale clause attached, you'll have to: a) Be prepared to qualify credit wise. b) Possibly pay a higher rate of interest if the existing rate is substantially below the market rate. c) Pay a substantial loan assumption fee. d) Pay a prepayment penalty when you sell. e) Be prepared to pay off the existing loan or get a new loan if the lender decides to exercise the due-on-sale clause.

GATHERING ALL THE DATA

At this point you have a particular property located which appears profitable; you have an appraisal (see chapter on appraisal), and have arrived at an upper and lower price range which you're prepared to offer. What now?

You will now have to research all of the following: name of the trustor, trustee, and the lender (beneficiary). Is it a first deed of trust in foreclosure or a second? When was it recorded and for how much? Is there a second trust deed in existence? If the second deed of trust is in foreclosure, who holds the first? Is it a conventional loan or a government backed loan which can easily be assumed?

In addition, you'll have to know how much the loan or loans are in arrears? If the taxes are delinquent, and if so for how much? What about other liens against the property?

Most of these questions can be answered in the office of the County Recorder where the subject property is located. All documentation involved with real property is kept open to the public in the County Recorder's office.

The recording process dates back to before the Civil War. Now as it did then, it provides to the public a notice of important documentation in regard to real property. When it comes time to develop data on a property in foreclosure, note that a first deed of trust recorded first has priority over those liens that are recorded subsequently. In other words, the first in line is first in right to any claims on the property, should a default occur.

The actual recording process is done by the County Recorder. When a deed is recorded, the beneficiary will submit a deed to the County Recorder, who files a copy of that deed in the official records.

CLOSING THE DEAL

In order for the distressed owner to be ready to make a deal, the following criteria must have been met before a transaction can take place. The owner has to be convinced that the investor is a knowledgeable specialist in the field of real estate. This will be accomplished by the investor during the initial stage of negotiations, when the investor portrays his acquired knowledge about the foreclosure process, revealing to the owner exactly what will occur if the condition is not remedied. The investor will additionally inform the owner that time is of the essence, that it is too late to list his property with a brokerage firm, or possibly it's too late to borrow additional funds. That by selling to the specialized investor now, the owner will relieve his distressed condition, salvage his good credit rating, and can leave the burdensome property behind with some cash in hand. Otherwise, the lender will acquire the property and everything will be lost, including his credit rating and all of his accumulated equity.

The distressed owner should feel that he appreciates the investor's interest in his predicament, and that help is near at hand. He feels he can speak openly, now that the limits of his financial difficulties are out in the open. And for that reason, the owner no longer feels someone is intruding and he doesn't have to disguise the facts about his troubled financial condition.

So now the distressed owner is prepared to act. Time is running out and he has been alerted of the consequences of his troubled situation. He knows that the investor can remedy the situation better and faster than anyone else. So now he is ready to make a deal.

As Time Passes . . . The Lower the Price

Time is money. In no other field of business can this truism be more emphatically stated. During the typical ninety-day span which a foreclosure proceeding takes, in which a property can still be reinstated, an offer to an owner during the first thirty days would be considerably higher than an offer made during the final days of redemption. During the final days of the redemption period the offer would be at its absolute lowest.

By the time a property reaches the final days of the ninety-day period of reinstatement, additional unpaid monthly installments have accumulated, and late charges have increased. The owner must be alerted to these facts, and that the quicker he acts to resolve his problem, the more he will get out of it.

MAKING SURE NAMES ARE CORRECT

It is absolutely imperative that the Seller(s) name on the Deed is correct and all the information on the deed transferring the property, is exactly like that on the original deed the seller received from the lending institution. If the seller's true legal signature is Andrew J. McLean, it is necessary to put down the name exactly as it is shown, not Andy McLean or A. McLean. Errors often occur when information is copied from published information services. Thus, always use the information which exists on the original grant deed.

Once the grant deed is signed over by the owner, it is important that you immediately take it to the recording office and have it recorded. After recordation, submit a copy of the grant deed to the title company. By immediately recording the grant deed, you can be assured that any liens recorded against your newly acquired property will be invalid, as long as they are recorded behind your name, and not before.

First you must have the seller sign the equity purchase agreement which will give you, the buyer, control of the subject property. This will be accomplished after completing final negotiations and checking that, in fact, the property is actually transferable. Then, the grant deed can be executed, signed by the owners and properly notarized. Again, be sure that the grant deed is filled out exactly as the previous grant deed. Once the grant deed is properly executed and notarized, it must be taken to the County Recorder for recordation. (See samples of various deeds at the conclusion of this chapter.)

PASSING TITLE INEXPENSIVELY

Before really digging in and discussing the various ways you, as an investor, can save costly charges associated with transferring real property, it will be to your advantage to familiarize yourself with local customs regarding this important matter. Again, I must state that local and state laws vary somewhat throughout the country, and for this reason it is difficult to be precise about legal customs in your exact area. Therefore, it will be to your benefit to discuss the basics of passing title with both a title officer from a local title company and the County Recorder.

Title companies will be happy to discuss procedures, especially if you in turn bring them your business.

EQUITY PURCHASE AGREEMENT

(This agreement to be filled out in triplicate, with a copy going to the seller, one copy for the buyer, and a copy for the buyer's file records.)

Date _____ Address of subject property _____
Lot _____ Block _____ Tract _____
Name of lender _____ Loan Number _____
Name of Seller _____ Address _____
Name of Buyer _____ Address _____

Buyer agrees to purchase and Seller agrees to sell the equity in the above described real property for the sum of _____ net to the seller, receipt of which is hereby acknowledged by the Seller.

Buyer agrees to take title to the above described property subject only to existing liens and encumbrances not exceeding _____ .

It is also mutually agreed that: _____

Seller is to deliver possession of subject property on or before _____, 19 ___ . If the property is not transferred to the buyer by the above agreed date, all payments and further expenses incurred from that date forward shall be deducted from the net amount to the Seller.

Buyer will pay all escrow, title, loan transfer, and closing costs.

Monthly payments on the above loan including principal, interest, taxes, and insurance are _____ .

Impounds for taxes and insurance, if any, are to be assigned without charge to the buyer. Any unforeseen shortage in the impound account will be deducted from the net amount due Seller at closing.

Seller will immediately execute a Grant Deed in favor of Buyer, which the Buyer has the right to record.

Seller will not remove any fixtures from the real property, and that he will leave property reasonably clean and in good condition.

Seller will allow Buyer access to subject property for any reason prior to date of possession of the Buyer.

Buyer will pay the balance of all funds due Seller at closing after checking title, loans, and liens, and the property is vacated.

Additions to this agreement: _____
_____
_____

Buyer _____ Seller _____
Buyer _____ Seller _____

GRANT DEED

RECORDING REQUESTED BY

AND WHEN RECORDED MAIL THIS DEED AND. UNLESS
OTHERWISE SHOWN BELOW. MAIL TAX STATEMENTS TO

NAME

STREET
ADDRESS

CITY
STATE
ZIP

TITLE ORDER NO   ESCROW NO

SPACE ABOVE THIS LINE FOR RECORDER'S USE

GRANT DEED

THE UNDERSIGNED GRANTOR(s) DECLARE(s)
DOCUMENTARY TRANSFER TAX is $ _____
☐ computed on full value of property conveyed, or
☐ computed on full value less value of liens or encumbrances remaining at time of sale, and

FOR A VALUABLE CONSIDERATION, receipt of which is hereby acknowledged.

hereby GRANT(S) to

the following described real property in the

County of _____ . State of California:

Dated _____

STATE OF CALIFORNIA
COUNTY OF _____ } ss.
On _____ before me. the
undersigned. a Notary Public in and for said State. personally appeared

_____ . known to me
to be the person _____ whose name _____ subscribed to the within
instrument and acknowledged that _____ executed the same
WITNESS my hand and official seal

Signature _____

(This area for official notarial seal)

MAIL TAX STATEMENTS AS DIRECTED ABOVE.

JOINT TENANCY GRANT DEED

RECORDING REQUESTED BY

AND WHEN RECORDED MAIL THIS DEED, AND UNLESS
OTHERWISE SHOWN BELOW MAIL TAX STATEMENTS TO

NAME

STREET
ADDRESS

CITY
STATE
ZIP

TITLE ORDER NO _____ ESCROW NO _____

SPACE ABOVE THIS LINE FOR RECORDER'S USE

JOINT TENANCY GRANT DEED

THE UNDERSIGNED GRANTOR(s) DECLARE(s)
DOCUMENTARY TRANSFER TAX is $_____
☐ computed on full value of property conveyed, or
☐ computed on full value less value of liens or encumbrances remaining at time of sale, and

FOR A VALUABLE CONSIDERATION, receipt of which is hereby acknowledged,

hereby GRANT(S) to

, AS JOINT TENANTS,

the following described real property in the

County of _____ , State of California:

Dated _____

STATE OF CALIFORNIA
COUNTY OF _____ } SS.
On _____ before me, the
undersigned, a Notary Public in and for said State, personally appeared
_____
_____
_____ , known to me
to be the person _____ whose name _____ subscribed to the within
instrument and acknowledged that _____ executed the same.
WITNESS my hand and official seal.

Signature _____

(This area for official notarial seal)

MAIL TAX STATEMENTS AS DIRECTED ABOVE.

QUITCLAIM DEED

RECORDING REQUESTED BY

AND WHEN RECORDED MAIL THIS DEED AND. UNLESS OTHERWISE SHOWN BELOW. MAIL TAX STATEMENTS TO

NAME

STREET ADDRESS

CITY STATE ZIP

TITLE ORDER NO _____ ESCROW NO _____

SPACE ABOVE THIS LINE FOR RECORDER'S USE

QUITCLAIM DEED

THE UNDERSIGNED GRANTOR(s) DECLARE(s)
DOCUMENTARY TRANSFER TAX is $ _____
☐ computed on full value of property conveyed. or
☐ computed on full value less value of liens or encumbrances remaining at time of sale, and

FOR A VALUABLE CONSIDERATION, receipt of which is hereby acknowledged,

hereby remise, release and forever quitclaim to

the following described real property in the

County of _____ , State of California:

Dated_____

STATE OF CALIFORNIA
COUNTY OF _____ } ss.
On _____ before me. the undersigned, a Notary Public in and for said State. personally appeared

_____ , known to me to be the person _____ whose name _____ subscribed to the within instrument and acknowledged that _____ executed the same. WITNESS my hand and official seal.

Signature _____

(This area for official notarial seal)

Title Order No. _____   Escrow or Loan No. _____

CHAPTER 3

Gaining Position of the Second Loan

Undoubtedly, investing in foreclosure property has recently become very popular among the public. Lectures, seminars, and various training guides have been made available to interested investors. Needless to say, this increase of informed foreclosure investors will add competition to available investments in the market. In order to head off at the pass most of the competition, it will be necessary for you to gain position of the junior financing. The best way to gain position of the second, or junior loans of record, which may appear while searching out title records is to buy them outright at a discount.

Essentially, two different types of secondary loans will prevail on a given property. The first is a "purchase money" loan, which is initiated by a seller of real property to assist the sale by carrying back a second loan. In other words, assume the seller of a home sells it to a buyer for $100,000. Terms are $10,000 down, $80,000 financed through a conventional lender, and the remaining $10,000 the seller carrys back in the form of a second trust deed.

The other type of secondary loan is the "hard money" second. This form of second loan is where the owner of real property takes out a second loan and receives actual cash dollars in return.

The differences between these two forms of secondary loans are critical to you when it comes time to deal with the holders of these notes.

The "hard money" lender is usually a sophisticated lender who is in the business of lending money. He is both willing and able to protect his investment and is prepared to take the property back through foreclosure, if necessary, should a borrower get behind in payments. On the other hand, the purchase money note holder is usually not so sophisticated. He didn't loan out actual dollars, as did the hard-money lender. He simply took back a note to facilitate the sale of his home. Now he has to move out of the neighborhood, or perhaps to another state, and is unable to efficiently oversee his investment. This makes him a likely candidate for you to buy his note at a substantial discount. Not so much because he lacks sophistication, but because he has moved away and probably has not received the last few payments due him.

Let's look at it from the purchase money note holder's point of view. He has carried back a note for $10,000 to facilitate the sale of his home and he now lives out of state. He has not received payments on the note in the past two months. Obviously concerned, he writes a memo to the note holder requesting the money past due. No response. So he telephones direct. But still no money. Then all of a sudden one day he receives a message from the first trust deed holder that the buyers have not made payments to them, and that they have no other recourse than to begin foreclosure proceedings.

Now, in order to protect their second loan position, the purchase money note holder must make up all payments in arrears on the first loan and begin foreclosure proceedings under their second loan. This unforeseen condition was totally unexpected, yet it happens quite frequently, especially to sellers who move out of state. And should they do absolutely nothing to resolve this precarious condition, the first note holder will continue with the foreclosure proceedings, and their second loan position will eventually be eradicated at the foreclosure sale. If this occurs, the entire amount owed on the second would most likely be lost.

Assume that the first note holder did in fact hold a foreclosure sale. What actually happens? If it is the first loan that is in foreclosure, then the sale eliminates any form of liens that were recorded after that lien which was recorded and foreclosed upon. If a property had four loans on it, and the first loan went to foreclosure, then both the second, third, and fourth loans are eliminated. On the same property, if the second loan went to foreclosure, then the third and fourth loans would be wiped out, while the first would remain intact. The only time a lien is not entirely wiped out is when a property goes to foreclosure sale, and the proceeds from the sale are over and above that which is needed to cure the loan in foreclosure.

In effect, then, the foreclosure sale essentially wipes out any liens that were recorded after that particular note which is being foreclosed upon. This includes abstracts of judgements. The actual sale originates an entire new chain of title. (Note: Sometimes federal tax liens and pending law suits are exempted from being wiped out in a foreclosure sale. If the Internal Revenue Service has a tax lien on the property, they have 120 days to redeem the tax lien.)

WHAT MUST YOU DO TO GAIN POSITION?

Assume you have located a property in foreclosure and you determine that it is the first deed of trust that is being foreclosed upon. You must now find out if there is a second deed of trust recorded against the property. This information is available at the County Hall of Records (County Recorder's office). Look for a second trust deed that has been recorded concurrently, recorded next, with the first trust deed.

A recorded document will usually have an attached address which will offer you a lead to the holder of that deed of trust. If the address is the same as the subject property, it means that at the date of recording the holder of the note was still living on the property, and then moved away at a later date. If he has already moved to a new address after selling the property, then he'll be easier to find, because his new address will appear on the records.

If the address given in the recordation is current, you're in luck. But if the holder of the note has since moved away, you must find him before anyone else. This is often a most burdensome chore, but must be done in order to gain control. If you don't gain control of the second, then you'll have to assume the second when negotiating with the holder of the first at full value. By negotiating with the holder of the second, you can discount it substantially and make a much better deal for yourself.

Okay, how do you find the holder of the second if his present address is not recorded? If he still lives in the same city he can be located by scanning the local phone books. If that doesn't prove fruitful, check the tax assessor rolls. If he owns any form of real property in that particular county, his name will appear along with his address or exactly where the tax bills are sent.

Assume that the tax assessor's rolls prove unsuccessful at locating the nomad. Now you can try the voters registry which is available to the public.

If he still can't be located, try mailing an urgent letter to the last known address, which is usually the address of the property being foreclosed upon. Request that the letter be forwarded. In the contents of the letter, make mention to the holder of the note that he can receive cash for his interest and for him to contact you immediately.

While you are waiting for a return from your written request, try getting information at the post office on a forwarding address.

Assume all the above methods prove unsuccessful at locating the now mysterious holder of the second deed of trust. You could pay a visit to the subject property and tell the owner that you're trying to locate "the nomad." You don't want the owners to know your exact intentions, just that it is urgent that you find the party which moved away.

Convincing the Note Holder to Discount

Convincing the note holder to discount is like preparing a legal defense case in court. You must make him aware of what he will face if the distressed owner does not make any further payments on the property. If the subject property progresses into further delinquency and the eventual foreclosure sale occurs, the second note holder will lose everything. If the second note holder decides to step in himself to salvage his position, he will have to do the following: bring the first loan in arrears up to date and assume control of the property. If he does this, he will essentially have to do the same things a specialty investor would do: refurbish the property, then sell or rent it.

On the other hand, if the second note holder made a reasonable settlement with you, the specialist investor, they would save time and effort, plus receive cash for their remaining interest in the troubled property. Very few people want to go through the hassle of a foreclosure action. Once payments from the troubled owner are a few months behind, the note holder may begin thinking how he can salvage some interest out of a precarious situation.

You must convince the note holder that you are in a better situation to resolve this deteriorating condition. Make it clear that it would be to his advantage to receive cash for his note, so the investor specialist can gain control of the property and, that the note holder would be required to make up back payments on the first loan to bring it current, then do costly repairs on the property, and devote much needed time and attention to rent out or sell the property, once control is attained.

Keep in mind that once a distressed owner becomes substantially behind in his payments to a second note holder, the holder of that note begins thinking in terms of what that note is really worth. Most of them would welcome some form of relief to salvage something out of a failing business deal. Once a note falls three or more months in arrears, most note holders would probably agree to accepting fifty cents on the dollar, or less.

CHAPTER 4
The Foreclosure Sale

Assuming you were unable to gain a second loan position, or you were unable to purchase the property outright prior to the sale, you still have an opportunity to bid on the property at the foreclosure sale.

At this point you should already have all the necessary information about the property. You know the exact condition of the loans outstanding, amount of unpaid taxes, if any, the estimated cost of refurbishment, and the fair market value of the property. This investment analysis you already made will be extremely helpful when it comes time to bid on the subject property.

An agent of the trustee will run the foreclosure sale. By this time the beneficiary has instructed the trustee as to what will be the opening bid. This figure will depend on the principal balance outstanding at the time of the sale, plus late fees, trustee fees, or the total cost involvement of the beneficiary. Most often, the opening bid, or minimum acceptable bid, will be the total amount owed to the beneficiary.

The minimum bid price is often contingent on the beneficiary's desire to own the property and how much equity remains in it. If the property is located in an extremely undesirable neighborhood with very little equity in it, the trustee may be instructed to reduce the minimum bid price below the amount owed the beneficiary in order to be sure of stimulating a sale. Or, in the case of a property having substantial equity, the minimum price offered may be increased, in order for the beneficiary to earn a profit at the foreclosure sale.

Possibly the best strategy on bidding at an open auction similar to a foreclosure sale is to be totally prepared. Know in advance how much you are prepared to bid and do not allow yourself to go over this predetermined price. You lose nothing if you don't buy at all. On the other hand, it is possible to get caught up in the frenzy of competitive bidding and pay much more for the property than you ever intended.

Those that hold the foreclosure sale will likely require that the bidders be prepared to pay for the property either in cash or cashier's check. Personal checks will not be accepted. The endorsers of personal checks can later stop payment, whereas cashiers checks are difficult to stop payment on.

Just prior to the sale, the holder of the auction will usually ask to see the money or cashier's check of those that will be bidding on the subject property. This is an attempt to qualify those that have an interest in the property, as opposed to those who might be in the arena merely as spectators. This will be the moment where you'll have a chance to look over those you will be bidding against.

Public foreclosure sales, astonishing as it may seem, attract many onlookers who have no intention of bidding. Of course, when the property involved has a very large first trust deed outstanding, the number of bidders will be restricted due to the greater amount of cash required to gain control. However, when it's a second or third trust deed being foreclosed upon, and the amount needed is small, there will of course be more bidders attracted to the sale.

In case of over-bidding . . . who gets the surplus proceeds? Assume, in this example, that the property goes to sale for $10,000, yet the auction continues and the final bid is made at $16,000, where does the extra $6,000 go? Everything over and above that owed to the lien holder that foreclosed goes to pay off the lien holders next in line. In this example, $6,000 would go to a second trust deed holder, then a holder of a third, if any of the $6,000 was still remaining.

Assume again in this example that you gained control of a second trust deed by purchasing it at a discount prior to the sale. Face value of the note you purchased is $8,000, however you purchased it at a discount for $2,000. Thus, when the final bid is made at $16,000, you would receive $6,000 with a built-in $4,000 profit. The only way you would receive the full $8,000 face value of the note is if the final bid price is $18,000 or more.

If there are any proceeds remaining from the sale after all lien holders have been paid off, it will go to the owners who lost the property in the foreclosure sale.

While you're in attendance at a foreclosure sale, be cautious of a bidder who may attempt to make a deal with you. Shrewd bidders prior to the sale have been known to pay off other potential bidders in an attempt to eliminate all the competition, so then they can purchase the property for the minimum bid price.

TALE OF THE FORTY THIEVES

During the mid 1970's in Southern California, the local media labeled a group of unethical foreclosure investors "The Forty Thieves." You may be familiar with the original Forty Thieves who existed during the era of Aladdin and his magic lamp. They roamed and pillaged the surrounding countryside, stealing anything that wasn't tied down. To avoid capture from their pursuers, this roving band would hide out in a cavern, concealed by a hinged cavern wall which would open on the command of "open sessame."

The forty thieves of the twentieth century are not exactly the thieves of yesteryear, although their clever unethical practices tend to relate them more with the likes of "Carpetbaggers" or "Robber barons."

These so-called forty thieves would show up at public foreclosure sales, appearing as individual investors unknown to each other. In reality, however, they were a band of investors with a prearranged plan of action. Prior to the actual sale, they determined which member of the group was to bid on the property being auctioned. The other members would buy off any apparent competition by paying them cash not to bid on the property. This, of course, would eliminate any competition, allowing the forty thieves to purchase the property at the minimum price.

CHAPTER 5

What To Do Once You Own the Property

We will assume that you now own the newly acquired property and you're thinking of investing in additional properties. At this point you have essentially three options available to you: 1) Sell at a profit, then reinvest the profits; or 2) Refinance your property and use the newly-borrowed money to purchase additional property; or 3) Trade your property, with additional capital, for one of higher value.

Now let us look at these options separately, noting their advantages and disadvantages. You will then make up your own mind which method serves your best interest.

OPTION 1: Sell at a profit, then reinvest the profits.

Advantages: Ideal for quick turnover on profits (i.e., rapid growth). Gives you experience at selling.

Disadvantages: A time lag can develop once the property is sold while you purchase another. Your initial profit from the sale is thus relatively inactive for a period of time, not earning the same return as if it were properly invested, and if it is your residence, you'll have to relocate.

OPTION 2: Refinance your property and use the newly borrowed money to buy additional property.

Advantages: Can lead to massive wealth, as continual reinvestment pyramids your investment without a time lag. If the original property is your own home, this saves cost and time of relocation.

Disadvantages: The only problem here would be that decreased earning capacity could make it impossible for you to make your increased payments. If you stay with property that has a positive cash flow, this difficulty is largely avoided.

OPTION 3: Trade your property for one of higher value.

Advantages: Zero time lag on invested capital. Also, and more important, the capital gains tax is deferred when you trade property for one of higher value (trading up), which means that whatever profit is gained, it continues to remain with your estate, growing with the rest of your equity. Eventually, if you sell, the tax must be paid, but you keep your profits on the use of that capital. This kind of transaction is referred to as a "tax deferred exchange."

LONG TERM CAPITAL GAIN: Tax Advantages

When an asset has been owned for a year or longer, then sold at a profit, only 40% of that profit is taxed by the Federal Government, and the maximum tax is 28% (no matter what the tax payer's bracket). Sixty percent of the profit is tax free. If an asset is held for less than a year, 100% of the profit on the sale is taxable as regular income.

You can see the advantages here immediately, but an example will show you how dramatic the difference is between capital gains and "straight income." If you sold a property, after owning it for 364 days, and made a profit of $10,000, if you are in the 50% tax bracket, your taxes would be half of the $10,000 or $5,000, and your remaining net profit would be $5,000. If you sell at the same profit after 366 days, your profit is $10,000 before taxes, but with capital gains only 40% of the profit is taxed. With capital gains you can only be taxed to a maximum of 28%, depending on your tax bracket. Therefore, in this example you would pay a maximum tax of $2,800 on the $10,000 gain. Your profit would be $7,200 with capital gains versus $5,000 without the capital gains advantage. By selling two days later, in this example, you increased your profits by a total of $2,200. With capital gains your net profit can be more than 44% greater than being taxed as normal income.

Further, if you as the seller decide to personally carry a secondary loan, where the buyer's down payment is less than 30%, you can distribute your profits proportionately over the period during which the loan is being paid off. This is why much real estate is sold at 29% down. (The rules on this subject are more complex than stated here. A detailed explanation of the tax laws which apply can be obtained by writing to the Federal Government.)

If as a homeowner you sell at a profit and reinvest that profit in another home, within one year from the date of sale, in a new home of higher value, the profit is not taxable. If however, you buy a new home for a lesser amount than the previous one, your profits on the first sale are taxable (as regular income or capital gains, depending upon how long you owned your original home).

For Those 55 Years or Older

As of 1979, Uncle Sam decided to deliver a nice birthday present to everybody over the age of 55 who owns his own home, and decides to sell it. In such a case, the first $100,000 in profit is absolutely tax free.

Some of the rules and exclusions governing this law are:

— You must have owned and lived in your principal residence for at least three of the five years preceeding the sale. There is an optional test for those 65 and older if they sell their homes before July 26, 1981.

— If you're married, only one spouse must qualify under the age, ownership, and residency tests.

— You can only take this exclusion once during your lifetime. Married couples are treated as one; if one spouse used the exclusion prior to marriage, the other spouse forfeits the right of the exclusion.

— The $100,000 limit is not cumulative. If you use $50,000 exclusion from the profit of one sale, the remaining $50,000 is forfeited and the unused portion cannot be used on the sale of another home.

WHEN TO SELL

Naturally, you would be foolish not to take the capital gains laws into account when you sell your property. You don't want to sell unless you've held it for a year or more.

But there are other considerations concerning time-to-sell which have a basis in the mathematics of equity growth. It is important to understand the principles involved here. As you will see, there is a point at which equity build-up causes the rate of return on your equity to diminish substantially below the rate of return you received during the early years of ownership.

Here, I will give you an example of equity buildup in a property of mine, showing the net income per year and the yearly rate of return on invested capital. From this example, you will be able to understand why it is necessary, at some point which you must determine through calculating your rate of return, to sell your property in order to keep earning a high growth rate on your investments.

I purchased an apartment building a few years ago for $110,000 with a $9,000 down payment, and $3,000 invested in improvements. Thus, my first year's equity position, before appreciation, was $12,000.

After a year, when all improvements were completed and rent increased, the fair market value of the property was $135,000. So, in the second year of ownership, my new equity position equaled the initial investment of $12,000, plus the increase in property value of $25,000, or $37,000.

Now, please refer to the calculations below to see how this increase in equity affected my rate of return on this investment:

Example of Diminishing Return of Equity Dollars.

First Year of Ownership

$110,000	initial cost of property
$ 9,000	down payment invested
+3,000	cost of improvements invested
$ 12,000	total investment, or equity first year
$ 5,400	first year net income
$ 5,400	divided by $12,000 (equity 1st year) = 45% return on equity first year.

Second Year of Ownership

$ 135,000   fair market value, 2nd year
−110,000   initial cost of property
─────────
=   25,000   gain in value, or equity
+   12,000   total investment, or initial equity
─────────
= $37,000   total equity, 2nd year
   $ 5,400   2nd year net income
   $ 5,400   divided by $37,000 (total equity 2nd year)
             = 14.6% return on equity 2nd year.

In the above example, note the diminishing rate of return on my equity from the first year to the second. The reason for this reduction is that my $25,000 profit, derived from improvements and appreciation, has not been reinvested. It is just "sitting there" as a paper gain.

To put it another way, this $25,000 is only "on paper." It is not "real" until I convert it to dollars and cents by using it, which I can do by selling the property (in which case the $25,000 will be in my pocket and I can reinvest it), or trading up.

Diminishing returns on equity must be considered when you are making decisions as to when to sell a specific property. It is often wise, once the property has reached the stage where you've derived a substantial profit from it, to sell or exchange it, to avoid the equity buildup which brings such dramatically reduced returns.

Selling the Property

Unless you are willing to do your homework and put in the time as well, it is probably just as well to pay a real estate broker a commission to sell the property and be done with it.

But if you decide you want to save the commission and have a go at it yourself, then this chapter explains the basic steps and considerations for accomplishing this.

Selling a property yourself is most sensible when the property is your own home (your principal residence), and when you are not in a hurry. If you have an extremely expensive property to unload, doing it yourself may take so long as to make it unprofitable in the long run. An exception to this is the story of a retired woman I know who put her home up for sale, handling the entire transaction herself, reaping the full profit of the sale worth in excess of one million dollars. That's the good part of this story.

The bad side of the tale is that it took her five years to find a qualified buyer. I hope you can imagine, with your new appreciation of real estate investment dynamics, how much more she could have made by selling that home in three months and paying the broker his commission.

However, $1,000,000 is a lot of property. The market for buyers in this price range, especially for single-family residences, is obviously severely limited, even in the plush area where this home was located. If you can carry some of the financing yourself, and your home can be purchased with a down payment which is low, relative to the average on the market, it may be worth your while to do the extra work and earn the commission yourself.

However, there is one observation before you proceed to do this. A real estate agent has hundreds of homes he can sell. He must still work very hard to make his income profitable. Many real estate agents put in 60 hours or more per week, including evenings and weekends. You have just that one home to sell, and unless your time is a fairly unimportant commodity, it might be better spent doing something else instead, while you pay a professional to sell your home and, at the same time, reap all the added benefits of his expertise.

Now that I've hopefully convinced you that it is not an issue of burning economic importance for you to go into sales on such a one-time venture, if you still want to go ahead with it, you may be handsomely rewarded.

The First Step: Determining Value

You can determine the fair market value of the property by yourself, following the suggestions in this text concerning the methods of appraisal. Or, you can hire a qualified appraiser, who can be found through inquiring at your bank or savings and loan, or simply looking in the Yellow Pages. The appraisal fee represents a sales cost which must be paid in this case.

Necessary Documents and Information

While you are figuring out what to sell the property for, you can also start obtaining the paperwork you will need, and getting questions answered concerning the status of your mortgages and other loans against the property

You need the following information from the carriers of your loans: 1) Is there a prepayment penalty on the loan, and if so, will they waive it if your buyer obtains his mortgage from the same lender? 2) What is the current principal balance on the loans? 3) Is there a tax and insurance impound account, and if so, what is the balance in the account?

Note that the prepayment penalty is a cost to you, levied by the lender according to the original loan agreement, charging you a penalty fee (6-months interest is common) for repaying the loan before it's due. This penalty charge covers the lender's cost in reclaiming and then reloaning the capital which you have paid back, and may be waived as noted above.

You will need the following documents:

— A copy of the paid tax receipt for the previous year.
— A copy of the survey of your property.
— Evidence of title.

Selecting an Attorney

If you do not already have an attorney for your real estate transactions, you should hire one to help you with the sale. Again, the attorney will have to be a real estate specialist, and should come well recommended, either by experience of friends, your loan counselor, or another attorney.

Since your attorney bases his charge on an hourly rate, you will save a lot of money by making sure he is completely supplied with all the necessary documents and information. If he charges $100 per hour (which is not unusual) and he must spend an hour making various phone calls and dictating letters requesting information and documents, that $100 comes out of your pocket. This kind of thing can be done by you personally. Every time you do something that saves your attorney time, you are effectively earning his hourly wage.

Your attorney needs:

— A copy of last year's tax receipts (if your lender does not have this, you can obtain it from the city or county treasurer).
— A copy of the title survey from the lender.
— A copy of your evidence of title, from the lender.
— Name, address and phone number of your present mortgage lender(s), plus the account or loan number of the mortgagor(s).
— Information regarding assessments, water and sewer provisions, and major repairs done recently.

These items are needed by the attorney in order for him to complete the sale on your property. Your attorney will further advise you as to what his function will be, what you must do to assist, and any other necessary details.

PREPARING THE PROPERTY FOR SALE

To get the most value from your property at the time of sale, it is essential that you tidy it up completely and do all the needed repairs. Cracks in the walls or windows, leaky faucets, and dirt all cost money. The property must be in spotless condition when you show it to a prospective buyer. And if your maintenance has not been taken care of, the prospective buyer will surely use this fact to reduce your asking price. So clean those windows and carpets, straighten out that messy garage, dust those window sills, polish the door knobs and get the cobwebs off the ceiling.

The Sales Information Sheet

This is a list of all the vital measurements and other information about your property, which you will distribute to prospective buyers. A sample copy of the Sales Information Sheet follows. Use a 50' tape measure to measure each room, and do this as accu-

SALES INFORMATION SHEET

Address _____ Selling Price $ _____

_____

Existing Mortgage Payment _____ _____ %

Architectural Style: _____   Const: _____   Basmt: _____

LR _____   Age: _____   Heat: _____

DR _____   Taxes: _____   220 wiring _____

Kit _____   Garage: _____   Water Htr _____

Dinette _____   Lot Size _____   _____

Fam. Rm. _____   Curbs & Gut. _____   Water soft _____

Other _____   Paved st. _____   _____

Bath _____   Sidewalk _____   Air Cond _____

Bath _____   Water _____   Schools _____

Bath _____   Sewer _____   High_____

Br _____   Septic _____   _____

Br _____   Grade _____

Br _____   _____

Br _____   Middle

Draperies & Curtains _____   _____

Carpeting _____

Items included: Oven _____   Range _____Ref. _____

TV Antenna(s) _____

Disposal _____D. Washer _____

Items not included _____

_____

Owner _____ Phone _____

rately as you can. Enter this and all other stipulated information on the sheet, and make copies which will be handed out to prospective buyers.

The "For Sale" Sign

The purpose of a For Sale sign is to advertise and locate your property. Unless your property is on a well-traveled thoroughfare you will need more than one sign. Count the number of turns a prospect has to make from a major thoroughfare in order to get to your property. That will be the number of additional signs you'll need. Then, get permission from the property owners where you want to place your signs, and order as many as you need.

All your signs will be 24" square with red (or green) and black letters on a white background. The sign in your front yard will read "For Sale—By Owner" in black, with your phone number in red or green. Additional signs to locate the property will look the same except a red or green arrow replaces the phone number.

Advertising

The purpose of your advertising is to get prospects interested enough in your property to come by and look for themselves. Place your ad in the classified section of your Sunday newspaper, because Sundays are when other realtors place their ads. Prospects are accustomed to looking for homes in the Sunday paper. (For additional information on writing ads, see Chapter on Property Management.)

SHOWING THE HOUSE

At this point you have an appraisal of your home and an attorney. The house is neat, clean and repaired. Your for sale signs are ready for use, and you have copies of the property information sheets to give to prospective buyers. Now prepare a guest register (a simple note pad will do) for incoming prospects, requesting name, address, and phone number. (The guest register is used by realtors to follow up on these prospects at a later date. However, as a homeowner, you can also use the guest list as a potential "suspect list," should any of your valuables be missing after your "open house."

Before preparing the house for showing, be sure the children and relatives are away from home so you won't have distractions when you are discussing business with potential buyers.

Now you can begin preparing the home so that it appears warm and comfortable. Turn off the television and turn on the radio to some soothing music. Light the fireplace and turn on all the interior lights to brighten and enliven the home as much as possible.

When to Show Your Home

Saturday afternoons and Sundays are customary days for "Open House," mainly because most buyers do their looking on the weekend, thus you take advantage of all the home buyers attracted to your area from other open houses being advertised.

THE SALES AGREEMENT

When a visitor to your open house says he is interested in purchasing your home, or that he wishes to sit down and discuss terms of the sale at your earliest convenience; what you have now is not a sale, but a serious and interested prospect. It is now time to negotiate and reduce the details of your negotiation to writing.

After all negotiations are in written form, have the buyer fill out a purchase agreement checklist, from which your attorney can draft the actual sales agreement which will be a legally binding contract, once both buyer and seller sign it.

The Purchase Agreement Checklist is used as a guideline in the preparation of documents for completion of the sale, and saves your attorney from having to spend unnecessary time asking questions.

PURCHASE AGREEMENT CHECKLIST

NOTE: Nothing should ever be signed by anyone until your attorney has approved it.

Name of prospective buyer(s) _____

currently residing at _____

_____ phone _____

are considering purchasing the property located at _____

_____

for a purchase price of $ _____

Earnest money deposit to be held by seller's attorney $ _____

Balance of cash (down payment) at closing $ _____

Amount of mortgage required $ _____

Type of financing _____

Interest at _____ % for a term of _____ years

principal and interest payments to be approximately $ _____

per month

Real estate taxes last year were _____

Contingencies to be included in purchase agreement _____

_____

_____

_____

_____

Items not included in selling price _____

Items that are included in selling price _____

_____

Sellers will vacate the premises on _____

Date of Closing escrow _____

Sellers to pay rent of $ _____ per day if sellers occupy premises after the close of escrow.

Legal description of property _____

_____

NOTE: This is not a legally binding agreement. It is simply a checklist to accommodate the drafting of a formal sales agreement between buyer and seller.

QUALIFYING THE BUYER

Just because you have a prospect who has announced his readiness to purchase your home, does not mean that you have a bonifide sale. Many a hopeful purchaser will nevertheless lack the ability to attain financing, in which case it is futile to enter into a sales agreement with him.

If your prospective buyer has already arranged his financing, or been told by a lender that he qualifies for a purchase in your price range, then it is not necessary to qualify him beyond getting proof of the above.

In all other cases, you must obtain the following information and qualify the prospect yourself, before you spend attorney fees formalizing an agreement that can never be consumated.

1. His employer's name and address.
2. Gross annual earnings.
3. Length of time with that employer.
4. Last year's total gross annual income.
5. His total liabilities.

If your prospect is married, you must get all of this information for both husband and wife.

Now, to determine a reasonable approximate monthly payment for the buyer (for principal, interest, taxes, and insurance), simply multiply the selling price of the property by 1%. The result will be a rough indication of what the payments will be, assuming a 20% down payment.

Now, to determine whether your prospect qualifies for financing at that rate, you can use the general rule of thumb accepted by the industry, which is that the payments should be no more than 25% of the combined gross income of both husband and wife. (Again, if there are very few liabilities, you can shade this up a bit to 33%.)

With a combined gross monthly income of $2,800 a reasonable payment would be 25% of $2,800, or $700. One percent of $70,000 is $700, so this income would qualify your prospect if your home is selling for $70,000 or less.

SUMMARY

We can now compare the total cost of sale "By Owner," to the cost of having the same property sold by a real estate broker who receives a 6% commission. Assuming a $70,000 home, the broker's commission would be $4,200 ($70,000 x 6%). When you deduct your own costs of sale from this amount, that will be your savings.

Appraisal fee: $50 to $200
Attorney fee: $40 to $100 per hour
"For Sale" signs: $20 to $80
Copies of property information sheet: $5
Total Cost: From $225 to $735

Thus, you will make from $3,465 to $3,945 (or save that much, if you look at it this way) by selling the property yourself.

CHAPTER 6
Appraisal

Once you have located a property that suits your particular goals and characteristics, it will be necessary to make an offer to the owner. The amount of this offer will depend upon many factors, but mainly upon appraised value of the property.

You could rely on a professional appraisal which would be a costly added expense. But if you are to be successful in real estate, it will be a good idea for you to be able to make rough appraisals for yourself. Such ability will be very handy later on, when it comes time for you to sell.

An appraisal of real estate is an opinion, or estimate, of the value of a property, made by gathering and analyzing the essential data as of a certain specific date. The appraisal is based upon the "highest and best use" of that property, that use which will produce the greatest net return. Such an estimate must take into consideration zoning laws, government regulations and the demand for that type of property in that area.

The appraisal of property is done by various methods, and the final opinion of value is given by weighing the values from each method used, i.e., by comparison.

Appraisal of real estate is an art, and not a science: the appraiser is actually arriving at a range of values wherein the subject property may be expected to sell. Although three different appraisers may arrive at three different opinions of value, each opinion will probably fall within a close range of value.

GENERAL FACTORS THAT INFLUENCE VALUE

The general factors which go into determining the value of a property are simply those of supply and demand. If land of that type is scarce or limited, the property values increase. A corollary of this principle is that value increases in areas of expanding population, or where the property has special attributes so that a larger number of people seek it out.

The utility, or usefulness of the property is then taken into account. I once saw a home that had been added onto in such a way that it was necessary to go through the kitchen and main bathroom in order to get to the master bedroom. This bizarre arrangement was obviously entered into as a way of making the improvements at a lower cost, but it also substantially altered the usefulness (and thus the appraised value) of that residence. Other such features, comical or otherwise, can affect the value upwards or downwards.

Finally, the transferability of a property will strongly affect its value. When a property is tied up in an estate, or is heavily encumbered with liens or other difficulties, a buyer may look forward to having his monies tied up in escrow for perhaps months, even a year or more. Such encumbrances substantially reduce the value of the property, since it cannot be easily sold at all.

SELECTIVE FACTORS INFLUENCING VALUE

Here we can make a list of certain "wanted" (or unwanted) attributes affecting the appraised value of any particular property.

- In a residential neighborhood, curving streets, cul de sacs, and uneven elevations of terrain, especially where this creates views, will tend to increase value.
- Proximity to such amenities as a lake, parks, shopping centers, schools and transportation will increase the value of residential homes.
- Fireplaces, patios, sundecks and views, tastefully color-coordinated interiors and exteriors and other such luxury items, will tend to increase the value of a single-family resi-

dence. In contrast, the absence of such qualities in an otherwise prime (high income) neighborhood may lower the value.

— Areas adjacent to manufacturing facilities and truck terminals tend to become slums eventually, reducing property value. Even before such deterioration takes place, the appraised evaluation is affected.

— Overcrowding of the land (i.e., buildings too close together,) where no plans have been made for grass and trees, is another situation which tends to breed decay. Such poor land usage eventually creates tenements where crime, arson and other threatening factors arise.

— In commercial or business property, the availability of parking, pedestrian count, traffic count, corner (versus midblock) location, and directional growth of the city will all affect the appraised value of a particular property.

METHODS OF APPRAISAL:
MARKET DATA APPROACH

There are three basic methods for appraising real property. The most widely used is the "market data" or "comparable sales" approach. With this method, recent sales of comparable properties in the area are considered and compared to the subject property, and the value is then adjusted upward or downward according to the amenities, construction type, quality and individual location.

A simple example of the comparable method approach would be to compare the subject property with three properties which have sold within six months and are located within the same housing tract, and are essentially without any meaningful differences. Assume all these comparables have sold for between 50,000 and 51,000 dollars, and that the subject property has a swimming pool while the comparables do not. You determine that a swimming pool is worth $10,000, therefore the subject property is worth about $61,000 ($51,000 + $10,000 for the pool).

For a more sophisticated example of the comparable approach, I have detailed on the following page all necessary adjustments in accurately appraising a single family residence. The description

EXAMPLE OF COMPARABLE SALES DATA

	SUBJECT PROPERTY	COMPARABLE 1		COMPARABLE 2		COMPARABLE 3	
		Descrip.	+–$adj.	Descrip.	+–$adj.	Descrip;	+–$adj.
Sales Price		$80,000		$81,000		$76,000	
Price/Living Area		$41.66 / sq ft.		$43.78 / sq ft.		$43.18 / sq ft.	
Date of Sale and Time Adjustment	Description	3 months	+1,000	3 months	+1,000	5 months	+1,500
Location					-1,000		+2,000
Site/View	Average	Average		good	-2,000	poor	
Design and Appeal	Fair	Fair		Fair		Average	
Construction Quality	Good	Good		Excellent	-2,000	Fair	
Age					-1,000		
Condition	Fair	Fair		Good		Good	
Living Area Room Count and Total	Total 6, Br 3, Baths 2	Tot 6, Br 3, Ba 2		Total 6, Br 3, Ba 2		Total 5, Br 2, Ba 2	+1,000
Gross Living Area	2,000 sq ft.	1,920	+2,400	1,850	+4,500	1,860	+4,500
Basement							
Functional Utility							
Air Conditioned							
Garage /Car Port							
Porches,patios, pools, etc.	Back patio	0	+2,000	0	+2,000	0	+2,000
Other; Fireplaces, Kit equip, remodeling		Fireplace	-1,000				
Financing Concessions							
Net Adjusted Total			+4,400		+2,500		+11,000
Indicated Value of Subject			$84,400		$83,500		$87,000

includes a dollar adjustment which reflects significant variations between the subject property and comparable properties. If a significant item in the comparable property is superior to, or more favorable than, the subject property, a minus (−) adjustment is made, thus reducing the indicated value of the subject; if a significant item in the comparable is inferior to, or less favorable than, the subject property, a plus (+) adjustment is made, thus increasing the value of the subject.

Reproduction Cost Method of Appraisal

The reproduction, or "replacement cost" method has three steps: 1. Determine today's cost of replacing all improvements on the property; 2. Deduct for all factors of depreciation to determine the current appraised value of the improvements; 3. Add the current improvements value to the value of the land. (The land is not depreciated since it is generally considered irreplaceable, indestructible and immovable.)

Let us assume that the subject property consists of a standard brick home on a 60' x 150' lot, and the home is 30 years old. If today's construction costs are $35 per square foot and your property contains 1500 square feet of living space, it would cost 1500 x $35 or $52,500 to replace the improvement. Now you must deduct the depreciation amount (see section on depreciation later in this chapter) from that cost. If depreciation amounts to $3,000, the current appraised value is $52,500 less $3,000 or $49,500. If comparable vacant lots (unimproved property) in that area are currently selling for $10,000, then your total appraised value of that property is $49,500 plus $10,000 or $59,500.

The reproduction cost method is predominantly used when appraising service properties, such as public buildings, schools and hospitals, and fairly new buildings of all types where the depreciation is a minor factor in the overall appraisal.

Capitalization or "Income" Method of Appraisal

This approach to the appraisal of real estate is primarily used to determine the value of income property. In order to understand this approach, we must first look at the entire subject of "cash flow"—your monthly net income from a property.

Cash flow comes in two forms: positive and negative. Defined, it is the amount of actual cash an investor will receive from property after deducting operating expenses and debt service (loan payments). Usually, the amount of cash flow an investor receives from a property will depend upon the down payment, or equity, invested in the property, and whether that property is considered prime or lower income.

For example, when I purchased my first income property, I ended up with a monthly cash flow of $102, based upon a 10% down payment. What this means is that when all my expenses, including taxes, insurance, loan payments and so on, had been paid out, I had $102 per month left as net profit. If I had put 20% down on that property, instead of 10%, my loan payments would have been less, which would give me more net profit or a higher monthly net cash flow. Thus, the more money you put into the down payment, the more cash flow increases in amount.

Another factor has a more practical aspect upon your effective income, and that is "risk." Because of the higher risk in low income or depressed neighborhoods, the rentals are proportionately higher compared to the value of the property itself, so that such property generates a much higher cash flow than prime property. Conversely, even with the 20% down payment, prime property in the best neighborhoods may actually generate negative cash flow . . . the gross income from the property will not cover expenses and debt service. If you rent a property for $500 per month, and your total monthly obligation towards that property is $550 per month, you will have to come up with $50 out-of-pocket to meet your obligations. That $50 is negative cash flow.

Obviously, positive cash flow is better than negative cash flow if you have a limited amount of working capital. But negative cash flow is not to be rejected out of hand, not when prime real estate is appreciating at 10% to 20% per year. That out-of-pocket expense will only last until the property appreciates and you can then raise the rent to cover your expenses, or else sell the property at a profit.

Now that we have a basic understanding of cash flow, we can

apply this to a further understanding of property values. The capitalization method of appraisal uses the net operating income to arrive at a fair market value for the property. However, in this case, the amount of down payment is irrelevant, since loan payments (and your income taxes) are not considered as expenses for purposes of this calculation.

This appraisal technique depends upon what the appraiser considers a suitable rate of return for investment capital in that area. Obviously, if you are investing in a high risk area, you must receive a higher return upon your investment. Conversely, prime property carries a lower risk factor and thus a lower rate of return.

This rate of return upon invested capital is called the "capitalization" or "cap" rate, and must be arbitrarily determined by the appraiser. The cap rate normally varies from 8% in the best neighborhoods to 12% in low income areas, but this percentage must be adjusted based upon the "going rate" for that type of property.

The appraiser determines the rate within the 8% to 12% range by considering the risk of the investment, along with the type of property and the quality of the income.

The net operating income (NOI) is used to determine appraised value using the capitalization approach. To arrive at net operating income, you will first calculate the gross income (based upon 100% rentals) and then deduct operating expenses, including potential losses from bad debts and vacancy losses. Again, your income tax upon earnings, and the loan payments, are not deducted from this figure. Property taxes are deducted, as well as management expenses, insurance, maintenance costs and repairs, replacement reserves, and so on.

If you want to appraise a property using this approach and you have calculated the net operating for that property as $25,000, while the cap rate for that type of property in that area is 10% (average), the appraised value would be $25,000 divided by 10% or $250,000.

If you will refer to the examples given at the end of this chapter, you will find that the sample Income Property Operating Statement (which contains all the information needed to calculate net income and cash flow) gives an example of a property with a net operating income of $31,994. Thus, the appraised value, using the capitalization approach, would vary from $266,617 (for a cap rate of 12%) to $399,925 (at 8%).

Appraisal by Gross Income Multiplier

This method of determining value cannot be classed as a professional approach, but it is often used as a quick off-the-cuff calculation, by brokers and in advertisements, for comparing like properties. You will often see income properties advertised in the newspaper, denoting a sales price as "eight times the gross." What this means is that the sales price of that particular property is eight times the gross income (income before deduction of expenses). For example, if gross income is $20,000, then the selling price would be $20,000 times 8, or $160,000.

This is a fast and simple method of determining an approximate value of a property, with respect to its gross income.

As with capitalization rate, the Gross Income Multiplier is determined by the appraiser within a range of values, taking into consideration the "going rate" for the area. This going rate is normally between 4 and 12, where the lower number represents the less desirable locations.

So if the Gross Income equals $20,000 per year:

Multiplier	Value
Worst area	=	4 times the Gross Income = $ 80,000 in value
Average area	=	7 times the Gross Income = $140,000 in value
Best Area	=	11 times the Gross Income = $220,000 in value

The Gross Income Multiplier is mostly used as an immediate gauge to determine whether a property deserves further attention. It gives only a ball-park estimate, it does not reflect net income, and is not a reliable rule of thumb for arriving at true market value.

DEPRECIATION

Depreciation must be understood and taken into account when making appraisal calculations. Depreciation is simply the loss of value of any asset for any reason, but in real estate it generally reflects the difference between the current value of a building improvement and its replacement cost at the time of valuation.

For income tax purposes, a depreciation allowance can be deducted from operating profits of income property. (This is where the term "tax shelter" came into existence. The owners of income property are sheltering, or protecting income through depreciation allowances.) Depreciation must therefore be taken into account when calculating net income and therefore appraised value of income property.

Essentially, any property held for the production of income can be depreciated, such as apartment buildings, rented homes, and whatever carpeting, furniture, appliances, and other equipment the owner may furnish.

Land is not depreciable. Therefore, to calculate depreciation on an apartment building, as we have said, the owner must determine how much of the total property value can be allocated to the building.

The most acceptable method is to use the latest tax bill on the property. The tax bill will note the assessed value for both the building and the land. Add the sums given for both, then divide the total into the amount allocated to the building alone. The result will be a percentage figure. Multiply the percentage figure by the price paid for the property and the result will be that portion of the total value of the property which can be depreciated.

Example to determine amount of depreciation

Assessed improvements	+	Assessed Land	=	Total Assessment
$50,000	+	$10,000	=	$60,000

Therefore: $50,000 divided by $60,000 equals .83 or 83%.
If you paid $250,000 for the property, then:

$250,000 x .83 equals $207,500 (value of the building, depreciable property).

Now that we have determined the amount which can be depreciated ($207,500), you must decide the remaining economic life, or useful life of the property.

Although the Internal Revenue Service has set various guidelines regarding useful life, for our purposes the following will suit most buildings:

1. Wood frame with brick veneer type buildings have a useful life of 30 to 35 years.
2. Concrete and block, 40 to 45 years.
3. Frame buildings, 25 years.
4. Brick buildings, 20 to 25 years.
5. Concrete and steel buildings have a useful life of 50 years.

Straight-Line Depreciation

This method offers an equal amount of depreciation each year over the useful life of an asset. If the depreciable property is valued at $80,000, with an estimated useful life of 40 years, then the straight line method will give a $2,000 per year deduction ($80,000 divided by 40 years equals $2,000) or 2.5% per year.

125% Declining Balance Depreciation

This method is for "used" residential income property, as opposed to brand new construction. It offers 125% (1.25) of the straight line deduction, but the increased rate is applicable only to the remaining balance each year, not to the original cost. This method results in higher deductions during the early years of useful life.

Using this method, the first year's depreciation is calculated at 125% of the straight line rate, or (for the property described in the previous example) 125 times $2,000 or $2,500..

The second year, depreciation is based upon the $80,000 cost minus the $2,500 already taken, or $77,500. The straight line yearly rate for this new value would be 2.5% of $77,500, or $1,937.50. Because you are using the declining balance method, you will now increase this deduction by a factor of 125%. Then $1,937.50 times 1.25 is $2,421.88 total depreciation for year number two.

150% Declining Balance Depreciation

This method is exactly like the preceding one, except that the larger rate of 150% is allowed on the declining balance. This method may only be used by an investor who qualified under the tax laws as "first user." This means either that the owner was himself responsible for the building construction, or else he acquired the building before the units were leased or occupied.

Sum of the Year's Digit Depreciation

This method is also available only to the "first user." Depreciation is calculated as follows: if the depreciable value of the property is $110,000, with a useful life of 10 years, the sum of the digits of those years (i.e., 1 plus 2 plus 3 . . . plus 10) or 55 is the denominator of your multiplier, and the number of years is the numerator. In this case, your multiplier is 10/55 or .18. This, times the original value of $110,000 is your depreciation for the first year. For year number two, 9/55 or .16 is used, for the third year 8/55, and so on.

INCOME PROPERTY STATEMENT

Location: 3756 S. Howard, Los Angeles, CA.
Description: 19-unit Apartment Building (4-1br, 14-2br, 1-3br).

INCOME GRID

No. of Units	Room Count per Unit	Description	Actual Rent per Unit	Total Monthly Rent
4	3	Unfurnished	170	680
14	4	"	210	2940
1	5	"	300	300

Gross Monthly Rent = $3,920

Annual gross income @ 100% = $3,920 x 12 = $47,040

Assessments: Land $10,000, Improvements $60,000

1. Gross Annual Income		$47,040
2. Vacancy and credit losses	2,352	
3. Taxes	4,834	
4. Insurance	940	
5. Utilities	1,800	
6. License & Advertising	200	
7. Resident manager	2,420	
8. Furniture & equip. Repl.	2,400	
9. Supplies	100	
10. Gardener & service maint.	0	
11. Services		
12.		
13.		
14.		
15.		
16.		
17. Total Expenses		– 15,046
18. Net Operating Income		31,994
19. Loan Payments (P and I)		– 18,000
20. Gross Spendable Income		13,994
21. Principal payment		+ 460
22. Gross Equity Income		14,454
23. Depreciation		– 15,000
24. Real Estate Taxable Income		(546)

Understanding the Income Property Statement

1. *Gross Annual Income:* Total annual rent the property would receive at 100% occupancy.
2. *Vacancy and credit losses:* Established by the "going rate" for similar properties in the neighborhood. Good areas are usually about 3 to 4%, while bad areas are as high as 10%. The national average is about 5% of gross annual income.
3. *Taxes:* Actual real property taxes for the current fiscal year.
4. *Insurance:* This is the total amount for all necessary forms of insurance. If the insurance is part of blanket coverage for several buildings, then you must adjust accordingly.
5. *Utilities:* A figure for a full-year operation including gas, water, and electricity.
6. *License and Advertising:* Use actual figures of advertising and license fee cost for entire year.
7. *Resident manager:* A total figure for the cost of the resident manager. Surveys indicate that a reasonable salary to pay a resident manager is a range of $5 to $17 per month per unit in the building. Professional management companies are paid a percentage of actual rents in addition to the cost of the resident manager. You can put any professional management fees in item *(11) Services.*

8. *Furniture and Equipment Replacement:* This item covers a reserve fund for replacement of furniture, drapes, carpets, and all major equipment (elevators, water heaters, etc.) 4 to 5% of gross annual income is a fair estimate.

9. *Supplies:* Rent forms, cleaning supplies, and all miscellaneous items are included in this category.

10. *Gardener and Service Maintenance:* Annual costs for gardening, pool cleaning, and maintenance, etc., are in this category.

11. *Services:* Professional management fees are placed in this category, not the cost of the resident manager. Professional management fees range from 5% to 10% of gross collected rents, depending on the size and character of the building. A minimum charge is made for smaller buildings.

12, 13, 14, 15, and 16 are reserved for additional expense items which may occur on various abnormal properties.

17. *Total Expenses:* Are total operating expenses before loan payments. As a rule of thumb, total expenses as a percentage of gross annual income should be in a range of 37% to 51%.

18. *Net Operating Income:* The result of deducting total expenses from gross annual income. This figure represents what the property would earn if purchased for cash free and clear of any loans. This item is also used to determine a capitalized value by dividing a suitable cap. rate in the Net Operating Income.

19. *Loan Payments* — including principal and interest. The annual total of payments is to be used under this heading.

20-24. This section of the statement shows potential earning capacity and cash flow before and after income taxes and depreciation.

INCOME & EXPENSE ANALYSIS

Property address: 3640 Raymond Av., Los Angeles, CA.
Description: 15-unit apartment building

INCOME GRID

(1) No. of Units	*(2)* Room count per unit	*(3)* Description	*(4)* Actual rent per unit	*(5)* Fair rent per unit	*(6)* Total monthly fair rent
3	2	Unfurnished	150	150	450
4	3	"	200	220	880
5	3	"	210	222	1110
3	4	"	250	270	810

Furniture value $ _____   Land value $ _____
Effective age   10 yrs. _____   Remaining life   40 yrs. _____
Rent $3,250 (multiply by 12 and enter on line 1 below)

ANNUAL OPERATING EXPENSE:		CAPITALIZATION PROCESS
Real estate taxes	$6,000	1. Gross Annual Income $39,000
Personal property taxes		2. Vacancy & credit loss
Insurance	700	@ 6% of annual gross 2,340
Electric	400	3. Gross Annual Effective Income
Water	480	(line 1 minus line 2) 36,660
Trash removal	600	4. Total Operating
Advertising	100	Expense 14,120
Gardening		5. Net Operating Income
Pool service		(line 3 minus line 4) 22,540
Prof. management		6. Capitalization: anticipated
Resident manager	2,640	rate of return 10.5%
Building Maintenance	1,600	7. Capitalized value of land
Replacement reserves	1,600	and building (line 5
Misc.		divided by line 6) 214,667
TOTAL OPER. EXP.	**$14,120**	Total Property Value = **$214,667**

CHAPTER 7

Property Management

Residential property management concerns itself with all aspects of advertising, leasing and maintaining your rental units. Most of the activities associated with property management can be turned over to a professional company. It is probably advisable for you to use such professional services when you own very large, multi-unit income properties, or if you simply prefer not to get involved in direct control of your real estate.

Professional management companies usually charge from 5% to 10% of gross collected rents for their services, except in the case of smaller or single family residences, where you will usually be asked to pay a flat monthly rate which varies with the size and character of the building.

The management company's responsibility is to operate your building, paying all expenses, and to send you a monthly report of its activities along with your reimbursement for any net proceeds.

Turning management responsibility over to a professional firm will, as we have said, cost you from 5 to 10% of your gross income. If you own 60-units with an average rental of $250 per unit, your gross collectable rent is approximately $180,000 per year (60 x 250 x 12 months), and you will pay 5 to 10% of that, or $9,000 to $18,000 per year "off the top," for professional services. As you can see from this example, property management is a flourishing business. If you have the time and inclination, and your holdings are relatively manageable, it will therefore benefit you to learn how to do it yourself.

EARLY MANAGEMENT DECISIONS

Furnished versus Unfurnished Units. During the past few dec ades there has been an industry-wide trend towards unfurnished units, mainly because people move less often when they have furniture to cart around, and this factor cuts down vacancy losses. For the same reason, furnished apartments attract a more transient class of tenant. Furthermore, if you as the owner, supply all the furniture, you have the additional expense of maintaining it.

The biggest exception to this general principle is with single or studio-type apartments, which attract mainly transient trade anyway. These are so difficult to rent unfurnished that it will pay you to furnish them.

Appliances. Appliances such as stoves, refrigerators and air conditioners are extremely expensive to maintain. For lower income units, I have found it advantageous not to supply any appliances whatsoever, since most lower-income families are accustomed to supplying their own. However, better quality apartments attract good tenants more readily when you furnish the appliances, and it usually pays to do so in such cases.

If you do decide to supply appliances, make sure the rent and deposit reflect this added service.

Utilities and Trash. In most buildings, especially newer ones, there are separate gas and electricity meters for each individual unit. The owner of the building pays the water bill.

When separate meters are available for gas and electricity, the owner must add utility costs to the rent, and then hope the tenants are efficient in their use of energy. If you own a building which lacks separate meters for each unit, it usually pays off in the long run to have them installed if you're planning on keeping the building for a long term investment.

Trash removal is best handled by the owner when multi-unit properties are involved. Your building must be kept clean, and the only way to avoid friction among the tenants as to who is responsible is to maintain control yourself.

Laundry. Should you install a laundry facility if you don't have one already? If so, should you buy or lease your equipment?

In most cases, with eight units or less in one complex, it is wise not to have machines at all. In smaller buildings, the washer and dryer will not be used enough to pay your utility expenses.

However, my experience with supplying laundry machines has been good. For instance, for one 19-unit family apartment building, I lease two washers and two dryers. The gross monthly receipts are between $200 and $280. Of this, the leasing company keeps 60% and reimburses me for the remaining 40% (which averages $80 to $112 per month). The leasing company maintains the equipment and collects all monies from the machines. I only pay the utility expenses to operate them.

Usually, with eight units or more, washers and dryers can be purchased outright, and will pay for themselves within two or three years. With fewer than eight units, laundry equipment is not a practical investment.

Needless to say, if you buy rather than lease, you will have expenses related to maintenance, not to mention possible losses due to vandalism and theft (from the coinbox).

If you do decide to lease laundry equipment, be sure that you or your resident manager are present during the removal of coins from the machines, so that the collection man will not be tempted to pocket a portion of your income. But if the resident manager and collection man are in cahoots, it is difficult to do anything about it.

Carpeting. Wall-to-wall carpeting does add a special glow of warmth and luxury to your units. Before you go overboard, however, you must consider expenses related to return-on-investment. Instead of installed wall-to-wall coverage, you can keep carpeting expense to a minimum by using linoleum in the entrance area and hallways, and at times in the dining area. Linoleum lasts much longer than carpeting and represents a significant savings in your original capital expenditure.

When you do purchase carpeting, a gold tweed shag of good quality is your best value. Gold tweed matches almost any furnishing colors, and shows stains less than other kinds. Furthermore, it is best to stay with one standard color for all your units, in order to take advantage of quantity discounts when purchasing. Shag carpet has an advantage over other types in being easier to patch, although it is more expensive to begin with.

The carpeting industry is highly competitive, and you will find that you have a large number of suppliers to choose from. Shop around and get the best price. And consider using the moonlighters of the industry who will often install a carpet for less than the cost of a package deal from a large supplier.

AVOIDING VACANCY LOSS

In order to maintain maximum income throughout the operation of your buildings, it will be necessary to keep vacancy losses at a minimum by reducing tenant turnover. Adequate maintenance is the primary way of keeping your tenants happy and satisfied. It cuts down on the inclination to move elsewhere.

You can thus keep good tenants by properly preserving the condition of your buildings. And this means being reasonable about requests and complaints. (Obviously, you cannot do much about keeping a tenant if his employer requests him to relocate.)

It is your responsibility as landlord to keep everything in good working order. At the same time, the tenant is responsible for not misusing the property he rents. Painting, carpet shampooing and plumbing are the owner's responsibility. When the tenant does things like pouring grease down the kitchen drain, causing continual stoppages, he and not the owner becomes responsible for the cost of repair.

About a year after he has moved in, a tenant will normally begin to request maintenance and/or refurbishment, assuming the unit was in excellent condition to begin with. A wall or two may need paint, new carpeting may be required, or perhaps only a carpet shampoo is in order. At these times, you can lose a good tenant if you do not respond reasonably (and pleasantly) to his needs.

If your tenant moves out because you were disagreeable, or because you wouldn't paint the kitchen for him, it will cost you more money in the long run, much more than the price of a paint job. You will not only have to prepare the unit for a new tenant, but you will also probably suffer revenue loss due to an unneeded interim vacancy. And, in order to attract a new tenant, you'll probably have to paint the kitchen anyway.

So take care of your investment. This will not only maximize your cash flow while you own, but more than that, it will allow you to present to future prospective buyers the most inviting spectacle in the neighborhood—a building full of happy tenants.

RENTING AVAILABLE UNITS

Here we will cover the step-by-step procedure for filling a vacant unit with a qualified tenant. Please note that I did not indicate that your goal is simply to get that unit rented. The fastest way to bankruptcy, not to mention migraine headaches, is to make a practice of renting to unqualified tenants, who will turn out to be nonpaying tenants. There are enough responsible prospects to fill your vacant units. If you rent to deadbeats, you'll end up wishing the unit was vacant in the first place.

Please believe me: filling up your building with unqualified tenants is a good way to attempt financial suicide, and is absolutely useless if you have any healthier purposes in mind.

Advertising. Getting prospects to your door is best accomplished using vacancy signs and classified advertising. Vacancy signs must be precise and to the point, and include enough information to qualify prospective tenants to a degree. For example, "Vacancy, 1-Bedroom, Adults Only," or "Vacancy, 2-Bedroom, Kids OK," gives such qualifying information. When you state such important facts you will eliminate having to spend time dealing with prospects who are looking for something you don't have.

Vacancy signs should be legible and large enough so that they can be easily seen from a passing car. Signs must also be placed where they get maximum exposure; either on the side of your building, or on the lawn nearest the busiest street. Classified advertising should also be precise and qualifying in order to cut down unnecessary calls.

Beyond these requirements, there are four basic principles of good advertising which you must keep in mind when you write your ads. These may be referred to as A.I.D.A.: Attention, Interest, Desire, and Action.

1. ATTENTION. Your headline should attract specific prospects. It could say "Newly Decorated" or "Large 2-Bedroom." The purpose of the heading is to gain attention by distinguishing your ad from the other ads in the same column.

2. INTEREST. An expansion of the headline should offer a benefit to the prospect, making him want to read the rest of the ad. Phrases like "New Dishwasher," "Newly Carpeted," and "Great Ocean View," will improve readership of your ads.

3. DESIRE. This is developed by descriptive copy which makes the prospect want what you have to offer. Some enticing phrases are "Kids OK," "Quiet cul-de-sac," "Olympic Pool," and so forth.

4. ACTION. When you ask for action with a classified ad, more prospects will respond. This can simply be accomplished using the word "call" followed by your phone number.

Classified ads are grouped (classified) under specific headings, and you do not need to duplicate this information in the body of your ad. For example, it is not necessary to state that your apartment is unfurnished when your ad is placed under a column headed "Unfurnished Apartments," or that you are located downtown when your classification already gives this information. Elimination of unnecessary verbiage saves money, because you pay for this type of advertising by the word or line.

Now that you have located your vacancy sign properly, and your classified advertising is running in the local daily newspaper, it is time for you to market your available unit to prospects. In order to do this successfully, you must be able to answer questions about the available unit, and be knowledgeable about the immediate area concerning schools, shopping, bus routes, etc.

If you have a resident manager for your units, you must make sure that he possesses this knowledge as well. Here is a checklist of information which should be at your finger tips and preferably, in your head:

INFORMATION ABOUT YOUR BUILDING

1. Size of the available unit, square footage, optional available layouts.
2. Size of individual rooms.
3. Closet space, linen space, cupboard space.
4. Equipment: refrigerator, stove, disposal, type of heating, air conditioning, furnishings.
5. Amenities such as pool, sauna, and so on.

INFORMATION ABOUT THE AREA

1. Income level.
2. Noise level.
3. Location of shopping centers.

4. Public transportation.
5. Highway routes.
6. Recreation areas.
7. Points of interest.
8. Educational facilities.

It is important that your vacant unit be immaculate. Dirt costs money. That empty unit will be much easier to fill when it appears bright, new, and most of all, clean.

If your units have certain disadvantages, don't expose them (or allow the manager to expose them) to prospects. A disadvantage to some people may not be so to others. Let sleeping dragons rest.

RENTING AN APARTMENT

After the manager has shown the prospective renter around the building, and the individual seems to be a likely candidate, unless the prospect has already said yes, the manager must tactfully request action. A good sales approach might be to say, "When would be a good time for you to move in?"

If the prospect decides to take the apartment, have him leave a minimum $75 deposit to hold the unit. This deposit commits the prospect, and reserves the unit. It has the further effect that, if your potential tenant has second thoughts overnight, he can often be resold when he returns to claim his deposit refund.

Once a deposit is accepted, you must have the prospect fill out a rental application. From this the prospect can be investigated, to see whether he qualifies. Do not rely on instinct.

I cannot say this too forcefully. In the rental business, there are many apartment owners and managers who will allow people to move into available units "off the street." When a complete stranger wants to rent from you, he is basically saying, "Give me the use of your $20,000 investment," or whatever the unit is worth. It is foolhardy to agree, without first investigating him, as though a complete stranger approached you on the street and asked for your car keys and you just gave them to him.

Time after time, tenants do acquire possession of assets worth tens of thousands of dollars, giving no more information than the fact that they need a place to live.

A tenant in possession, whether or not he decides to pay the rent, has the legal right to use and enjoy your property without being disturbed. Removing such a deadbeat from your premises must be done by due process of law. In California this is an unlawful detainer action, and in most other states you must file an eviction suit. But these actions, if successful, only bring a judgement for rent monies, court costs and moving fees. Cases that go to court can require twenty to thirty days or more to settle, and the costs involved, plus additional rent loss, can get way out of hand, especially if a professional deadbeat who knows all the "angles" decides to slither onto your premises and not pay his financial obligations.

The only way to avoid this sort of calamity is to check prospective tenant backgrounds. This can be done either by joining a local apartment house association (which offers such services) or by checking with past landlords and verifying employment and references supplied on the rental application.

LEASE AGREEMENTS

The relationship between owner and tenant is created, operated and terminated under very specific laws in each state. You will be primarily involved with fixed and periodic tenancy.

Fixed tenancy means tenancy for a specific period of time (such as one year.) It specifies an exact starting date and duration, and is not renewed or extended without agreement by both parties. Rent payments do not necessarily coincide with the term of the tenancy. Thus, if a tenancy is for one year, rent is still normally paid on a monthly basis during that year.

Periodic tenancy involves a continuous series of specified terms, which are automatically renewed unless one of the parties gives notice to terminate. An example would be a typical month-to-month agreement where occupation of the premises runs for one month and starts over again, successively running for another month. Rent is usually paid by the month, as well. With periodic tenancy, unless a tenant gives notice or is asked to vacate, tenancy is automatically renewed when the owner accepts the rent.

Technically, a lease is an agreement between a tenant (lessee) and owner (lessor) whereby the tenant agrees to pay a specific rental on a certain property for a specific period of time. In addition to being a contract, a lease is a conveyance or transfer of property rights, and it must contain the following: form, intention, delivery, and term (beginning and ending dates).

Some states allow verbal leases. However, I recommend your leases all be in writing. The lease is useful in case you have legal difficulties, and it enables you to contractually prevent the tenant from subletting.

Every state sets different limitations, but in general a lease must be in writing if it exceeds a specific term, usually one year. Similarly, the transfer or assignment of a lease to another tenant (subletting), for a term of one year or longer must also be in writing. Terms of a written lease can only be changed or modified by another agreement in writing.

The lease spells out the agreement between the two parties to the lease, and must contain provisions for subletting by the tenant, public liability, and the responsibilities of both parties regarding losses due to fire, earthquake, etc.

A lease signed by the owner (lessor), when delivered to the tenant (lessee) becomes binding when the tenant moves in and pays rent, whether the tenant signs it or not.

When a lessee abandons the property during the term of a lease, he is not released from his obligation. Lessor may sue for rent as it becomes due. If lessor rents to another party, he can only recover his actual losses from the breaker of the lease.

Death by a lessee or lessor does not cancel the lease, which is binding upon the heirs. If the lessee dies, the lessor can file a rent claim against the deceased's estate.

Lessee is required to take "reasonable care" of the property, unless the lease requires him to keep it in a specified condition.

A lessee may sublet all or part of the property, often for a higher rental, unless a provision in the lease prevents this. When a subletter sublets in turn to another tenant, he is said to hold a "sandwich lease."

A *Percentage Lease* is a special form generally used for retail business, where a percentage of the gross sales is used to determine rent. A minimum base rent is stipulated by the lessee, to cover periods of reduced sales. Sometimes, such leases are structured as "triple net leases," wherein the tenant is responsible not only for paying the owner a percentage of net income, but also for real estate taxes, insurance and maintenance.

Signatures on the lease. A lease must be signed by tenant, tenant's spouse, and all adults who will occupy the premises. Where two, three or more are sharing an apartment, a clause of "Tenants are jointly and severally responsible for payment of rent," is required.

If the resident manager signs a lease for you as the owner, the signatures should appear as follows: John Doe (Owner) and James Jones (Manager).

In order to be legally binding, a lease must be delivered, and must show the following:

1. Complete legal names of all parties involved.
2. That it is intended to be a lease, and that it establishes an owner/tenant relationship.
3. A complete description of the premises.
4. Amount of rent to be paid, and when it is due.
5. Term of the lease (one year, month-to-month, etc.).

If the tenant remains on the premises after expiration of the lease, and if the owner accepts rent, tenancy becomes periodic month-to-month or week-to-week.

Usage and custom in the United States have established that rents are paid in advance. They are normally due at the end of each previous payment period, unless otherwise stipulated in the lease.

Subletting. A tenant may assign or transfer his lease to another party unless your lease contains a clause preventing this. Your lease should specify that subletting may not be undertaken without written consent of the owner.

Existing Tenants. When you take over management of a building, be sure all existing tenants are under some form of written agreement. If not, make appointments with them and have them sign a new rental agreement. In the case of furnished units, you will also want to make an inventory of all furniture during the visit, and have the inventory signed as well as the new rental contract.

Deposits. Apart from rent, certain deposits will be necessary before right of possession is confirmed. A security deposit is a refundable deposit protecting the owner from damage to the premises caused by the tenant. A good rule of thumb in a month-to-month tenancy is to charge one month's rent as a security deposit. This amount can be adjusted upwards, depending on the value of the apartment and other amenities you might offer, such as a stove, or refrigerator and air conditioner.

Prior to move-in, tenant should be informed that the security deposit cannot be applied to his last month's rent when he vacates, but will be held until after the apartment is vacated, with proper notice and is in reasonably good condition.

Another necessary deposit is the nonrefundable cleaning deposit. This charge normally runs in the range of $50 to $100, depending on the character and income level of the tenants. Certain states disallow cleaning fees, in which case you can simply rename the cleaning fee to a "one-time leasing charge," nonrefundable.

A key deposit is necessary. It is refundable when the unit is vacated and the key(s) returned. A reasonable sum to charge is $10.

Additional deposits should be required if you allow pets on the premises. One hundred to $200 is suggested as a deposit for pet damage.

RENT COLLECTION

Profitably managing your real estate invariably depends on your collection policies. A good collection policy begins by properly qualifying the tenant before he moves in. Then, before you give out keys and hand over possession, you must collect all deposits and rent in advance. There is absolutely no excuse for relaxing these requirements.

Your apartment building or home for rent is purely a money-making business, not the Salvation Army. You're not running a mission for charity. Owners who yield to deadbeats not only end up in bankruptcy, but they also make it possible for such scoundrels to exist! You're not being a good-guy when you allow someone to hoodwink you—you're just making it that much easier for him to go on plying his trade.

Rents can be collected efficiently when the resident manager and tenants are aware of all your collection procedures, and know that these procedures are followed and upheld. A good policy is to have all rent-due dates effective within the first seven days of the month. Exceptions can be made to accommodate paydays.

Effective, professional contract forms should be used. A triplicate rent receipt form is necessary, with a copy for the tenant, if he wants it, the resident manager, and a third copy for the owner. A reminder notice should be used when rent is three days past due, and given personally to the tenant, or placed upon his door. If there is no response to the reminder notice, the manager must make a personal visit to collect. If no progress is made in this way, the three-day "Pay Rent or Quit the Premises" notice must be issued immediately (see The Eviction Process which follows for further details).

Many sophisticated property managers charge a ten dollar late fee when rent is more than three days past due. Others offer a ten dollar discount if the rent is paid within three days of the due date. Some states do not allow the practice of charging late fees, but most allow the discount as an incentive.

Another helpful approach to rent collection is the "Delinquent List." This is simply a sheet of paper listing tenant names, due dates, and rental amounts, with a column for comments. At the beginning of each month, the manager lists the tenants, then crosses out each name as the rent is paid. Occasionally, a tenant will be late and tell the manager that the rent will be paid on a specific date in the near future. This date would be noted in the "comments" column and crossed off when the payment is made, or followed up if not. Also in the comments column will be information as to when late notices were given to the tenant, and follow-up procedures that have been utilized. With this delinquency list, both owner and manager can check up on the status of rental collections at a glance each month.

When a tenant has established a good payment history, more lenient allowances can be made, especially in such situations as loss of a job, illness or a death in the family. Whatever the case, a definite commitment must be made and recorded on the delinquency list, and followed up by the manager.

Rent payment must be made in the form of a check or money order. *You should not accept cash.* This eliminates temptation of theft, or the impulse on a manager's part to borrow from the till. Only in an emergency, or when a tenant is extremely late in paying his rent, should cash be accepted.

THE EVICTION PROCESS

The following explains the step-by-step procedure for legally evicting a tenant in the case of non-payment of rent. This procedure may vary slightly from state to state:

1. Tenant is served with a "Three Day Notice to Pay Rent or Quit the Premises" when the tenant is more than three days delinquent.
2. If, after this three days, no rent is received and the tenant stays on and does not quit the premises, an "Unlawful Detainer" is filed with the Municipal Court and a Summons is issued.
3. The Summons and Complaint is served on the tenant, who then has a right to file a plea and an answer to the Complaint. If this occurs, a trial will be held, otherwise:
4. Default of the tenant is assumed by the court, which then issues a Default Judgement.
5. The court issues a Writ of Possession to the Sheriff or Marshall.
6. The Sheriff or Marshall evicts the tenant (physically or otherwise).

Occasionally it will be necessary to evict a tenant for other reasons than non-payment of rent, such as unauthorized pets, too much noise, or too many people living on the premises. To evict under these circumstances, you must serve the tenant with a 30-Day Notice to Terminate Tenancy. If the tenant moves out within the prescribed thirty days, there is no need to proceed further. If, however, the tenant remains on the premises after the prescribed thirty days, you must begin with procedure no. 2 under the Eviction Process, and follow all the subsequent steps.

HOW TO RAISE RENTS

At the initial stage of taking over management responsibility for a building, it will usually be necessary to raise the rents of most of the units. Rental increases for existing tenants are handled the same as any other change in the terms of tenancy. In most states the law requires a minimum 30-day notice of a rental increase.

When increasing rents, some tenants may decide to move rather than pay the higher rate, especially if they can find less expensive comparable housing in the same immediate area. It is therefore important that you keep rent raises on a par with comparable housing in your area. Tenants will then be likely to remain to avoid the cost and inconvenience of moving.

To avoid having a large number of vacant units at one time, do not send out rent raises to the entire building at once. Raise no more than 25% of the building in any single month, until you have all the units at comparable rates. The best time to raise rent is when a vacancy occurs.

Please note that under specific lease agreements rents cannot be raised during the term of the lease, but only upon its expiration.

THE RESIDENT MANAGER

Once a property is purchased and basic improvements and rental increases accomplished, an apartment owner has to allocate only a few hours of his time per month to any individual property if he delegates authority to a resident manager. With a competent resident manager on the premises, you are relieved of many time-consuming operations and responsibilities. On the other hand, an incompetent manager can be a needless expense, a headache, or (usually) both.

In order to have your operation going so efficiently that you need spend only a few hours per month on a property, you must give as much responsibility as you possibly can to the manager, making only major decisions yourself. Then, you can devote your time to policies involving your entire estate, and concern yourself with the more challenging aspects of property ownership rather than burdensome daily chores.

When you acquire a property, you must decide whether to keep the existing resident manager or find a new one. Usually, thirty days is time enough to determine the capabilities of the existing manager. Then, should you be dissatisfied, look for a replacement immediately, because good managers are plentiful, as you will discover.

Certain qualities make for a good resident manager, and a husband and wife are ideally suited for the job. The husband usually works full time at a regular job while the wife is free to manage. After the husband comes home from work, he can then do minor maintenance and repair work. The following are qualities you should find in a good resident manager, listed in order of importance.

1. Eagerness and willingness to do the job well.
2. The ability to accept responsibility.
3. A husband who is handy at minor repairs.
4. A wife with a pleasing personality and a willingness to stay home and perform routine management duties.
5. Honesty.
6. Experience.

Please note that "experience" is listed last in priority. Many times I've found that it takes more effort to weed out so-called experienced managers and their inefficiencies than it does to train a new, inexperienced person.

Primarily, the manager's responsibility is to collect rents, show vacant apartments, and keep the grounds clean. A husband, who may have a full-time job elsewhere, can operate as handyman for minor repairs and lawn mowing, or other yard work. It is important not to have to call in skilled labor every time there is a minor repair job to be done.

The manager must be on the job to show vacancies and keep order during the day. A wife who is overly active outside the home is not a good prospect. The domestic housewife with children tends to be the best "stay-at-homer."

What you pay the resident manager depends primarily on the size of the building to be managed. With a twenty-unit complex, free rent is a typical agreement. On a small fourplex type building, twenty-five to thirty-three percent of rent on a one bedroom apartment is normal. Buildings larger than twenty units usually will offer the manager free rent, plus a cash salary. Look in the classified section of your local newspaper under the heading "Couples Wanted" to find competitive rates and salaries in your area.

SUPERVISING THE RESIDENT MANAGER

Duties of the resident manager must be fully explained at the beginning of the employer/employee relationship. Remember, the more responsibility you can delegate, the more time you will have to pursue other matters.

A monthly report is a necessity for accounting, and ready for reference. This report should include a list of rents collected, one copy of the triplicate rent receipt, a delinquency list, and a bank deposit receipt. Larger buildings require other types of reports noting vacancies, future available apartments, and so on.

The list of monies collected should include apartment number, date of payment, due date, amount paid, and purpose of payment (rent, cleaning, security fee, etc.). One copy of each triplicate rent receipt is attached to the collection sheet and given to the owner for his records. The resident manager also keeps on file copies of rent receipts, and the tenant receives the third copy, if requested.

Bank deposit copies, or reports, are optional, depending on whether the manager or the owner makes the bank deposits.

Monthly supervisory visits by the owner are a good practice. You can make major decisions regarding needed maintenance at this time, while inspecting the common area and picking up collected rents.

On the following pages are sample management forms.

RENTAL APPLICATION

Last Name _____ First _____ Initial _____

Spouse Full Name _____

Unit to be occupied by _____ persons.

Present Address _____City _____

State _____ Zip _____ How Long _____ mo's _____ yr's

Applicant's birth date _____ Driver's Lic No. _____

Soc. Sec. No. _____ Spouse birth date _____

Drive Lic. No. _____ Soc. Sec. No. _____

Present Landlord _____ Phone _____

Monthly Pymt. _____ How Long _____

Previous Landlord _____ How Long _____

Employer _____ How Long _____

Address _____ Position _____ Salary _____

Closest Relative _____ Address _____

City _____ State _____ Phone _____

Bank _____ Check Acct. No. _____

Credit reference _____ Acct. No. _____

Credit reference _____ Acct. No. _____

Vehicle No. 1 _____ Lic. No. _____

Vehicle No. 2 _____ Lic. No. _____

Name & address of referring party _____

_____

Signature of applicant: _____

Date: _____

MONTH-TO-MONTH RENTAL AGREEMENT
(SAMPLE)

This is intended to be a legally binding agreement. Read it carefully.

Dated _____ 19 _____

_____ California

1.   _____ Landlord (lessor), agrees to rent to
_____ Tenant (lessee), the premises described
as _____
_____ together with the following furniture and
fixtures _____
_____

(If list is extensive, attach hereto as exhibit "A.")

2.   The rental shall commence on _____ 19 _____,
and shall continue month-to-month unless otherwise stated here:
_____

This rental may be terminated at any time by either party by giving written
notice 30 days in advance, unless a longer or shorter period of advance notice
is specified here: _____
_____

Tenant agrees to pay $ _____ rent per month on the
_____ day of each month. When rent is paid on or before the due date,
Tenant may take a $ _____ discount. The security deposit on the
dwelling unit is $ _____ and it is only refundable when the dwelling
is left undamaged. A deposit of $ _____ for _____ keys will
be refunded after the keys have been returned to landlord.

Landlord will refund all refundable deposits within 14 days after tenant
has moved out completely.

3.   Tenant agrees to pay upon execution of this agreement, in addition to
rent, a nonrefundable one-time leasing charge (or cleaning fee if legal) of
$ _____ .

4.   Tenant agrees to pay all utilities except _____ which shall
be paid for by the landlord.

5.   Tenant has examined the premises and all furniture and fixtures contained therein, and accepts the same as being clean and in good order, condition and repair, with the following exceptions: _____
_____
_____

Month-to-Month Rental Agreement (continued)

6. The premises are rented for the use only as a residence for _____ adults and _____ children.

No animal or pet except _____ shall be kept on the premises without the Landlord's prior written consent.

7. Tenant may not assign, transfer, or sublet to another person without the written consent of the Landlord.

8. Tenant shall not disturb, annoy, endanger or inconvenience other tenants of the building or neighbors, nor use the premises for any immoral or unlawful purposes, nor violate any law or ordinance, nor commit waste or nuisance upon or about the premises.

9. Tenant shall obey the rules and regulations for the property attached hereto.

10. Tenant shall keep the premises rented for his exclusive use in good order and condition and pay for any repairs caused by his negligence or misuse or that of his invitees.

11. With tenant's permission, Landlord shall be permitted to enter to inspect, to make repairs and to show the premises to prospective tenants or purchasers. In an emergency, Landlord or his agent may enter the premises without securing prior permission from tenant, but shall give tenant notice of such immediately thereafter.

12. Tenant shall neither paint nor make alterations of the property without Landlord's prior written consent.

13. If tenant abandons or vacates the premises, Landlord may at his option terminate this agreement, re-enter the premises and remove all property.

14. The prevailing party may recover from the other party his costs and attorney fees of any action brought by the other party.

15. Either party may terminate his agreement in the event of a violation of any provision of this agreement by the other party.

_____   _____
Landlord/Manager   Tenant

SAMPLE LEASE

This is intended to be a legally binding agreement—read it carefully.

Dated _____ 19 _____
_____, California.
1. _____Landlord (lessor), and _____
Tenant (lessee), agree as follows: Landlord leases to Tenant and Tenant hires
from Landlord those premises described as: _____

_____

together with the following furniture and fixtures: _____
_____ . (If list is extensive, attach hereto as Exhibit "A".)
2. The term of this lease shall be _____ commencing
_____ 19 _____ and terminating _____ 19 _____
3. If the tenant remains in the premises after the lease expires, and the landlord accepts rent, tenancy is changed to the term for which the rent is paid,
becoming a periodic tenancy of month-to-month.
4. Tenant agrees to pay rent as follows: _____

_____

When rent is paid on or before due date, Tenant may take a $ _____
discount. The security deposit on the dwelling unit is $ _____ and it is
only refundable when the dwelling is left undamaged. A deposit of $ _____
for _____ keys will be refunded after the keys have been returned to the
landlord. Landlord will return all refundable deposits within 14 days after
tenant has moved out completely.

NOTE: The remainder of the provisions in this lease can be duplicated from
the MONTH-TO-MONTH AGREEMENT beginning with provision 3.

IN CONCLUSION

Real estate in distress will offer the alert, well prepared investor, many golden opportunities to enhance his standard of living, or more important, a means to becoming financially independent. Not only will the knowledge and experience gained in this text help you with foreclosure property, but additionally it will be beneficial in more common real estate investments. This is due to the fact that in order to profitably and effectively acquire distressed real estate, much analysis and research is required. This experience will inevitably carry over enabling you to have more expertise at buying and selling real estate which is not in distress.

Primarily, I reveal my experiences with foreclosures relevant to the California market. Unfortunately, laws and customs in California do not dictate local ordinances throughout our country. So again, I would like to emphasize that in order for you to function efficiently in your own state, be sure and acquaint yourself with local ordinances regarding passing title and the overall foreclosure process. This could eliminate costly mistakes and misunderstandings between you, the seller, and lenders.

The future of real estate will inevitably supply the specialized investor boundless properties to acquire and refurbish, then either rent or sell his acquisitions at a substantial profit. Although at times the overall supply may be restricted during good economic climates, an adequate supply will return once the economy sours during a recession.

And, as a specialized distressed real estate investor, you can eventually emulate the great real estate tycoons of our country—those that were self-made and began with one property, then parlayed that initial property into a fortune in income producing real estate. This phenomena of building a massive estate from one seemingly insignificant property is not to be scoffed at. It happens time and time again, and to make it even more appealing, it's probably easier to do today then it ever was. This is primarily due to the skyrocketing rate of inflation, which causes real estate values to soar dramatically. And those who own the land will prosper significantly.

Skyrocketing inflation also aids the specialized investor. Because he can acquire a distressed property with the previous low interest loan attached. Thus, he not only purchases a property which will appreciate, he also acquires a valuable loan with an interest rate that is likely far below market rates of interest.

And so as time goes on, and our economy swings like a pendulum from boom to bust, homeowners will continue to allow their homes to go into foreclosure. Those that are knowledgeable and prepared to meet the opportunities available during these times will be assured of handsome rewards. Perhaps those rewards will be in the form of a home, which can be fully refurbished and comfortably lived in as a sound investment. Or, in the case of a more aggressive investor who seeks real estate investment as a full time career, his reward will be acquiring numerous profitable potential tenements, then completely refurbishing them, converting the one-time eyesores into projects that are considered the pride of the neighborhood.

Whichever the case, people will continue to buy and sell real estate, as they have done for centuries, and to those that endeavor to invest in the almost limitless real estate market, especially the unique foreclosure market, this handbook is sincerely dedicated.

GOOD INVESTING . . . Andrew James McLean.

DEED OF TRUST AND RENT ASSIGNMENT

RECORDING REQUESTED BY

AND WHEN RECORDED MAIL TO

Index as Trust Deed and Assignment of Rents and as Request for Special Notice.

— SPACE ABOVE THIS LINE FOR RECORDER'S USE —

DEED OF TRUST AND RENT ASSIGNMENT (SHORT FORM) ADDITIONAL ADVANCE

This DEED OF TRUST, Made this .... day of .... ,19 , between

.... , herein called TRUSTOR,

whose address is ....
(Number and Street) (City) (Zone) (State)

.... , a California corporation, herein called TRUSTEE, and

.... , herein called BENEFICIARY,

WITNESSETH: That Trustor irrevocably grants, transfers and assigns to Trustee in trust, with Power of Sale, the following described real property in the State of California, County of

TOGETHER with the rents, issues and profits thereof, subject, however, to the right, power and authority hereinafter given to and conferred upon Beneficiary to collect and apply such rents, issues and profits.

FOR THE PURPOSE OF SECURING:

1 Payment of the indebtedness evidenced by one promissory note of even date herewith executed by Trustor in favor of Beneficiary or order in the principal sum of $

2. Performance of each agreement of Trustor contained herein or incorporated by reference

3. Payment of such additional sums as may hereafter be borrowed from Beneficiary by the then record owner of said property, when evidenced by another promissory note (or notes) reciting it is so secured.

TO PROTECT THE SECURITY OF THIS DEED OF TRUST, TRUSTOR AGREES: By the execution and delivery of this Deed of Trust and the note secured hereby, that provisions (1) to (5), inclusive, of Section A and provisions (1) to (10), inclusive, of Section B of the fictitious deed of trust recorded in the book and at the page of Official Records in the office of the county recorder of the county where said property is located, noted below opposite the name of such county, viz.

COUNTY	RECORDING DATE	BOOK	PAGE	COUNTY	RECORDING DATE	BOOK	PAGE	COUNTY	RECORDING DATE	BOOK	PAGE
Alameda	8 7 78	RE 5521	IM 112	Napa	12 24 64	713	269	San Mateo	8 7 78	HEEl 7788	HNG 2414
Contra Costa	8 16 78	8970	46	Orange	1 2 63	6379	931	Santa Clara	3 31 71	9251	740
Fresno	8 4 78	7089	441	Riverside	11 30 64	3864	139	Santa Cruz	7 28 78	7878	698
Kern	8 4 78	5129	2143	Sacramento	8 7 78	78 08 07	1135	Solano	11 18 64	1307	56
Los Angeles	10 16 61	12044	401	San Bernardino	11 30 64	6787	186	Sonoma	12 24 64	7098	78
Marin	4 4 64	1879	58	San Diego	11 30 64	Series 5, Book 1964, Page 1366		Trinity	3 11 71	145	544
Monterey	2 28 78	1221	163	San Francisco	12 28 64	A860	900	Ventura	91 30 64	2678	2678

(which provisions, identical in all counties, are printed on the reverse hereof) hereby are adopted and incorporated herein and made a part hereof as fully as though set forth herein at length, that he will observe and perform said provisions, and that the references to property, obligations, and parties in said provisions shall be construed to refer to the property, obligations, and parties set forth in this Deed of Trust

THE UNDERSIGNED TRUSTOR requests that a copy of any notice of default and of any notice of sale hereunder be mailed to him at his address hereinbefore set forth

In accordance with Section 2924b, Civil Code, request is hereby made by the undersigned TRUSTOR that a copy of any Notice of Default and a copy of any Notice of Sale under Deed of Trust recorded .... in Book............ Page .... Official Records of .... County, California, as affecting above described property, executed by .... as Trustor in which...................................... is named as Beneficiary, and. .... as Trustee, be mailed to .... whose address is ....
(Number and Street) (City) (State) (Zone)

STATE OF CALIFORNIA ⎱ ss
COUNTY OF _____ ⎰

Signature of Trustor

On _____ before me, the undersigned, a Notary Public in and for said State, personally appeared

_____

. known to me
to be the person _____ whose name _____ subscribed to the within instrument and acknowledged that _____ executed the same
WITNESS my hand and official seal

Signature _____

If executed by a Corporation the Corporation Form of Acknowledgment must be used

(This space for official notarial seal)

NOTE SECURED BY DEED OF TRUST

INSTALLMENT NOTE — INTEREST ONLY

$ _____ _____, California, _____, 19 _____

In installments as herein stated, for value received, I promise to pay to _____ _____, or order,

at _____

the sum of _____ DOLLARS,

with interest from _____ on unpaid principal at the rate of _____

per cent per annum, payable in installments of _____ Dollars

or more on the _____ day of each _____ month, beginning on the

_____ day of _____, 19 _____

and continuing until _____ at which time the entire

principal balance together with interest due thereon shall become due and payable.

Should default be made in payment of any installment of principal or interest when due the whole sum of principal and interest shall become immediately due at the option of the holder of this note. Principal and interest payable in lawful money of the United States. If action be instituted on this note I promise to pay such sum as the Court may fix as attorney's fees.

Note Secured by Deed of Trust (page 2)

_____, California

_____, 19___

For value received, I hereby transfer and assign to

the within Note and the Deed of Trust securing the
same, so far as the same pertains to said Note, without
recourse. _____

Interest to accrue from

_____

By _____

PAYMENTS

DATE PAID			DATE DUE			Amount Paid	Interest Paid To	CREDITED ON		Balance Prin. Unpaid	To Whom Paid
M	D	Y	M	D	Y			Interest	Principal		

104

ASSIGNMENT OF DEED OF TRUST (INDIVIDUAL)

WHEN RECORDED, PLEASE MAIL THIS
INSTRUMENT TO

Order No. ....
Escrow No. ....

────── SPACE ABOVE FOR RECORDER'S USE ONLY ──────

ASSIGNMENT OF DEED OF TRUST (INDIVIDUAL)

(ASSIGNOR)

FOR VALUE RECEIVED, do   hereby grant, assign, and transfer to

all beneficial interest under that certain deed of trust dated
executed by   , Trustor

to   , Trustee
and recorded as Instrument No.
on   , in Book   , Page   , of Official Records
in the office of the County Recorder of   County, California,
together with the note or notes as therein described or referred to, the money due and to become due thereon with
interest, and all rights accrued or to accrue.

Dated ....

....

....

STATE OF CALIFORNIA
COUNTY OF _____ } SS.

....
On ...., before me, the undersigned, a Notary Public in and for said County
and State, personally appeared ....
known to me to be the person(s) whose name(s) is (are) subscribed to the within instrument and acknowledged that ....
executed the same.
(Seal)   ....
                                        (Notary signature line)
                                        ....

FULL RECONVEYANCE

RECORDING REQUESTED BY:

_____

AFTER RECORDING MAIL TO:

_____
_____
_____

————————————ABOVE SPACE FOR RECORDER'S USE————————————

FULL RECONVEYANCE

_____ , as Trustee under Deed of Trust,
dated_____, 19____, made by_____
_____
_____
Trustor; and recorded as Instrument No. _____ on_____, 19____,
in Book _____ , Page _____ , of Official Records in the office of the County Recorder of
_____ County, California, describing land therein as

having received from holder of the obligations thereunder a written request to reconvey, reciting that all sums secured by said Deed of Trust have been fully paid, and said Deed of Trust and the note or notes secured thereby having been surrendered to said Trustee for cancellation, does hereby RECONVEY without warranty, to the person or persons legally entitled thereto, the estate now held by it thereunder.

IN WITNESS WHEREOF, _____ , as Trustee, has caused its corporate name and seal to be hereto affixed by its Assistant Secretary, thereunto duly authorized.

Dated: _____

STATE OF CALIFORNIA } ss.
COUNTY OF _____

_____ ,
as Trustee

By_____
Assistant Secretary

On _____ before me, the undersigned, a Notary Public in and for said County and State, personally appeared _____ known to me to be the Assistant Secretary of the Corporation that executed the within instrument known to me to be the person who executed the within instrument on behalf of the Corporation therein named, and acknowledged to me that such Corporation executed the within instrument pursuant to its by-laws or a resolution of its Board of Directors.

WITNESS my hand and official seal.

Signature_____

_____
Na   (Typed or Printed)

(This area for official notarial seal)

NOTE SECURED BY DEED OF TRUST

DO NOT DESTROY THIS ORIGINAL NOTE: When paid, said original note, together with the Deed of Trust securing same, must be surrendered to Trustee for cancellation and retention before reconveyance will be made.

NOTE SECURED BY DEED OF TRUST
(INSTALLMENT — INTEREST INCLUDED)

$ _____, California, _____, 19____

In installments as herein stated, for value received, I/we, jointly and severally, promise to pay to _____ _____

_____

_____

or order, at _____ the sum of
_____ DOLLARS

with interest from _____ on unpaid
principal at the rate of _____ per cent per annum; principal and interest payable in installments of _____
_____ DOLLARS

or more on the _____ day of each _____ month, beginning on the _____
day of _____, 19 ____, and continuing until _____

Each payment shall be credited first on interest then due and the remainder on principal; and interest shall thereupon cease upon the principal so credited. Should default be made in payment of any installment when due the whole sum of principal and interest shall become immediately due at the option of the holder of this note. Principal and interest payable in lawful money of the United States. If action be instituted on this note I/we promise to pay such sum as the Court may fix as attorney's fees. This note is secured by DEED OF TRUST to   a California corporation, as Trustee.

_____   _____

_____   _____

ALL INCLUSIVE PROMISSORY NOTE SECURED BY LONG FORM ALL-INCLUSIVE DEED OF TRUST

DO NOT DESTROY THIS ORIGINAL NOTE: When paid. said note. together with the Deed of Trust securing same. must be surrendered to Trustee for cancellation and retention before reconveyance will be made.

ALL INCLUSIVE PROMISSORY NOTE SECURED BY LONG FORM ALL-INCLUSIVE DEED OF TRUST
(Installment Note, Interest Included)

$_____ _____$. California. _____ . 19_ .

In installments as herein stated. for value received. I We ("Maker") promise to pay to _____

("Holder") or order. at _____

the principal sum of _____ DOLLARS. with interest

from _____ on unpaid principal at the rate of

_____ per cent per annum; principal and interest payable in installments of _____

on the _____ day of _____ 19 _____ . and continuing until said principal and interest have been paid.

Each installment shall be applied first on the interest then due and the remainder on principal; and interest shall thereupon cease upon the principal so credited.

The total principal amount of this Note includes the unpaid principal balance of the promissory note(s) ("Underlying Note(s)") secured by Deed(s) of Trust. more particularly described as follows:

1. (A) Promissory Note:
   Maker: _____
   Payee: _____
   Original Amount: _____
   Date: _____

   (B) Deed of Trust:
   Beneficiary: _____
   Original Amount: _____
   Recordation Date: _____
   Document No.: _____ Book _____ Page _____
   Place of Recordation: _____ . County. California

2. (A) Promissory Note:
   Maker: _____
   Payee: _____
   Original Amount: _____
   Date: _____

   (B) Deed of Trust:
   Beneficiary: _____
   Original Amount: _____
   Recordation Date: _____
   Document No.: _____ Book _____ Page _____
   Place of Recordation: _____ . County. California

(A) Presentment. notice of dishonor. and protest are hereby waived by all makers. sureties. guarantors and endorsers hereof This Note shall be the joint and several obligations of all makers. sureties. guarantors and endorsers. and shall be binding upon them and their successors and assigns.

(B) To the extent that payments are required under the existing deeds of trust or the notes secured thereby for the purpose of creating and maintaining a fund for payment when due of taxes. assessments. insurance premiums or any other purposes. the Maker shall pay said installment payments to the Holder of this note in addition to the principal and interest payments due hereunder.

(C) During the term of this note. the Holder hereof shall pay all installments of principal and interest and other installment payments and charges due pursuant to the Underlying Notes but only from and to the extent of the payments received by the Holder from the Maker under the terms hereof. The foregoing obligation shall in no event include. with respect to the Underlying Notes. any penalty or premium. or any amounts required to be paid in addition to principal or interest (except as otherwise provided herein) or any installments of principal or interest which become due by acceleration unless such penalty. premium. other amount or installment are paid by the Maker to the Holder. Any such penalty. premium or other amounts required to be paid as a direct result of the Holder's failure to perform its obligation hereunder shall be paid by Holder.

(D) Should the Holder default in any payments due pursuant to the Underlying Notes. said payments having been received by Holder from the Maker. subsequent payments due under said notes may be made by the Maker directly and such payments shall be credited to this note.

(E) In the event of a default under the terms of this note. and a foreclosure under the terms of the All-Inclusive Deed of Trust securing the same. all demands for sale. delivered to the Trustee on foreclosure. shall be reduced by the amount of the unpaid balance. if any. of principal and interest on the amounts due on the Underlying Notes existing at the time of the Trustee's sale upon such foreclosure. provided that satisfactory evidence of such unpaid balance shall be submitted to the Trustee prior to sale by the Holder of this note.

(F) Notwithstanding anything to the contrary contained herein. or in the All-Inclusive Deed of Trust securing this note. the Holder of this note shall have the right to require full payment of any sums due hereunder whenever any senior underlying encumbrance shall become due and payable.

108

All Inclusive Promissory Note (page 2)

(G) Should default be made in payment of any installment or other sum when due the whole sum of principal and interest shall become immediately due at the option of the Holder of this note. If action be instituted on this note, the Maker promises to pay such sum as the court may fix as attorney's fees.

_____   _____
(Maker)   (Maker)

The undersigned hereby accept(s) the foregoing All-Inclusive Promissory Note and agree(s) to perform each and all of the terms thereof on the part of Holder to be performed.

Executed as of the date and place first above written.

_____   _____
(Holder)   (Holder)

(THIS NOTE IS FOR USE ONLY IN CERTAIN TRANSACTIONS. IT IS RECOMMENDED THAT, PRIOR TO THE EXECUTION OF THIS NOTE, THE PARTIES CONSULT WITH THEIR ATTORNEYS WITH RESPECT THERETO.)

INDEX